THE SHOOTING SCRIPT

SALTWATER

SCREENPLAY
AND POSTPRODUCTION NOTES BY
CONOR McPHERSON

THE NHB SHOOTING SCRIPTS SERIES

NICK HERN BOOKS
LONDON
www.nickhernbooks.co.uk

The Shooting Script Series

The Shooting Script Series was originally devised by Newmarket Press

The Newmarket Shooting Script Series is a registered trademark of Newmarket Press,
a division of Newmarket Publishing & Communications Corporation

This book first published in Great Britain and Ireland in 2001
as an original paperback by
Nick Hern Books Limited, 14 Larden Road, London W3 7ST

A CIP catalogue record for this book is available from the British Library

ISBN 1 85459 491 5

Typeset by Country Setting, Kingsdown, Kent CT14 8ES
Printed and bound in Great Britain by Hobbs the Printers Ltd,
Totton, Hants. SO40 3YS

THE NHB SHOOTING SCRIPT SERIES
I Went Down
The Ice Storm
The Shawshank Redemption
The Truman Show

For information on forthcoming titles, please contact the publishers:
NHB, 14 Larden Road, London W3 7ST

SALTWATER

screenplay
by
Conor McPherson

For Emer Reynolds

Note
Ringed numbers in the margins of the screenplay relate to
Conor McPherson's Postproduction Notes at the end of the book.
Square brackets in the screenplay indicate speeches or scenes
that were omitted from the final version of the film.

Conor McPherson, author and director

1. EXT. A SEASIDE TOWN IN THE TWILIGHT

A distant bell. A low foghorn. The rattle of cable on flagpoles. It's out of season.

2. EXT. A TAKEAWAY FISH & CHIP SHOP TWILIGHT

The shop is on the seafront. Above it is a flat. The shop is closed. There is some light in the flat.

3. INT. LIVING ROOM NIGHT   ①

GEORGE BENEVENTI (fifties, thin), his sons, FRANK (early twenties, athletic), JOE (sixteen), daughter CARMEL (late twenties, pretty) and her boyfriend RAY (thirties, a little overweight, striking) are playing poker around a table.

The characters emerge out of the gloom. They are half lit. We see them all separately when we like, as if we're at the table. They play for two pence pieces which they call 'units.' RAY is dealing a hand. He has only a few twopences left. The others all seem to have loads. They all drink beer, except for GEORGE who drinks whiskey and JOE who drinks coke.

                        GEORGE
            Who's shy? Who's shy?

The other BENEVENTIS join in, going 'Who's shy? Who's shy?'

                        RAY
            Oh. Sorry.

He puts four pence in the middle of the table.

                        GEORGE
            Nice ones now, Ray.

                        RAY
            I could do with giving myself a few
            nice ones.

                        FRANK
            You're after giving me a hand of feet.

5

                    CARMEL
          I hope no-one can open.

                     JOE
          I can't open but I'll play.

                    CARMEL
     Ray?

                     RAY
     Nah . . .

They're all about to fold but:

                    GEORGE
          Ah sure, it's open.

GEORGE opens for twopence. Everyone else goes 'Bollocks' or shakes
their heads with disappointment. 'Fuck's sake.'

                    GEORGE
          Oh, can-opener . . .

                     RAY
          Can I get a beer, Frank?

                    FRANK
          In the fridge. Help yourself.

                     RAY
     Anyone else?

Everyone raises their glasses, while discarding unwanted cards.

                     RAY
          Stupid question . . .

                    FRANK
          (Will) . . . I deal for you, Ray?

                     RAY
          Yeah. Give me three. Surprise . . .

RAY goes out. PAUSE. The others all start cheating.

                    CARMEL
          What's he got? Quick.

FRANK looks at RAY's cards, and starts laughing.

                    FRANK
          Two clubs. He's going for a . . . flush . . . ?

                      6

GEORGE
Quick, come here, give him three Jacks
or something.

JOE
This is mean.

GEORGE
And give me three Queens.

They are laughing. They desperately search through the deck.

JOE
I have a Jack, here.

4.   INT. KITCHEN NIGHT

RAY is lit by the fridge as he leans in, getting beers out.

5.   INT. LIVING ROOM SAME

FRANK gives GEORGE three Queens from the deck.

GEORGE
Now. Are we right?

FRANK
Yeah. Stop. Shh. He's coming.

They all sit quietly, barely containing their mirth. RAY comes in giving
them their drinks.

FRANK
Come on, we waited for you.

CARMEL
Who's it to?

JOE
Dad opened.

GEORGE
Oh, can opener. I'll have to make it . . .
ah, I'll let yous in. Three . . . units.

He puts 6p in the middle.

JOE
Three younits. Nah, I'm gone.

He folds.

FRANK
I'll have a look.

He puts in 6p.

                    CARMEL
          Gone.

She folds.

                     RAY
          Three units. Three younits. Ah sure,
          you'd nearly have to see that.

He puts in 6p.

                     RAY
          . . . With three.

He puts in another 6p. Everyone goes 'Ohh. Oh ho.'

                     JOE
          To you, Dad.

                   GEORGE
               (Examining RAY)
          The philosopher enters the real world, ha?

                     RAY
          I'm saying nothing

                   GEORGE
          Poker face.

                   CARMEL
          Poke her boobies, see if she's alive.

                     RAY
          Where did you get her from?

                   GEORGE
          We don't know, but we're trying to give
          her to you. We'll have a look.

He puts in 6p.

                    FRANK
          I'll have a look as well.

He puts in 6p. GEORGE winks at FRANK.

                   GEORGE
          Ah, you'd nearly have to.

                     RAY
               (Laying down his hand)
          Well. I had fuck all. And I bought in
          one, two, three little Jackaroonies.

CARMEL

Oh my God. He won a hand!

GEORGE

Looks like your luck is changing . . .
For the worse . . . De duh . . .

GEORGE shows his three Queens. RAY throws in his cards.

RAY

Ah, for fuck's sake . . .

GEORGE

(Reaching for the pot)
Popular win. Popular win.

FRANK

Well. It might have been.

GEORGE

Ha?

FRANK lays down three Kings, one by one.

FRANK

Three wise men. Bearing gifts.

GEORGE

Do you know what you are? You're a
little bollocks. Do you know that?

CARMEL, FRANK, and JOE are laughing.

GEORGE

If you can't play without cheating, you
just shouldn't play.

RAY

Here, wait . . . Were yous cheating?

TITLE SEQUENCE:

6. (1) INT. CHIPPER EARLY MORNING

This is a chipshop take-away restaurant. There are a few tables. It all looks
a bit rundown, worn. Needs refurbishment. The chipper is not open for
business. We track around. There is a take-away part and a sit-down part.

7. (2) INT. BEDROOM MORNING

FRANK and JOE share a bedroom. We track around the room while they
sleep. Among their odds and ends are some photographs, including a

9

picture of their mother, and a photograph of an attractive girl around FRANK's age. Beside which is a postcard denoting Chicago city. Over FRANK's bed are shelves full of war books, crime books, gangster videos and westerns.

8.   (3) INT. BEDROOM 2 MORNING

RAY and CARMEL are in bed together. She is asleep. He is watching her sleep.

9.   (4) INT. BEDROOM 3 MORNING

GEORGE lies asleep. [A bottle of whiskey near the bed.] He too has a picture of his wife, FRANK, JOE and CARMEL's mother. He also has her photograph on a memorial card.

10.   INT. BEDROOM 1 MORNING

An alarm goes off. FRANK stops it.

                    FRANK
            Joe. (Pause) Joe, come on.

As Joe wakes we see a flash of his dream. Just a second. A soundless home-movie feel with explosive colours. A woman on a beach with bare feet and a vivid red summer dress. She smiles. She wears dark glasses. This is the past.

                    JOE
            Yeah?

                    FRANK
            Get up.

[11.   EXT. STREET MORNING   ②

FRANK stands alone on the street outside the chipper, smoking, taking in the grey morning.]

                TITLE BOARD: 'MONDAY'

12.   INT. KITCHEN MORNING

FRANK cooks some breakfast. His appearance is neat. His demeanour regimented.

13.   INT. CHIPPER MORNING

It's not open for business. JOE and RAY sit with dirty plates. FRANK and CARMEL clear up. JOE is in his school uniform.

                    RAY
            (Conspiratorially)
        I love this.

                    JOE
        What . . .

                    RAY
        I love being in here before yous are
        open.

                    JOE
        Why?

                    RAY
        I don't know. No-one else can come in.
        It's like a little fucking . . . privilege.
        I like sneaky things. Do you know what
        I mean?

JOE smiles.

                    RAY
        I love anything sneaky.

JOE looks at a book RAY has on the table. It has a picture of an elderly
man and reads 'WOLFGANG KONIGSBERG. COLLECTED PAPERS,
1950-1980.'

                    JOE
        Who's that?

                    RAY
        Konigsberg . . . one of the world's most
        eminent philosophers. Visiting our
        college. Where I'm going to take him
        down a peg . . . or two.

                    JOE
        How are you gonna do that?

RAY taps his temple and winks.

                    RAY
        With this. You back in school today?

                    JOE
        Yeah.

                    RAY
        Yeah? You don't like it?

                    JOE
        Nah, it's boring.

11

> RAY
> Yous don't have a bit of doss?

> JOE
> Nah, there's loads of assholes in it.

> RAY
> The herd.

> JOE
> What?

> RAY
> They're like cattle, or sheep.

> JOE
> They're just dicks.

RAY laughs. JOE gets up.

> JOE
> I'll see you later.

> RAY
> I'll see you.

14.   INT. BEDROOM 3 MORNING

FRANK brings a tray with a cup of tea and some toast in to GEORGE.

> FRANK
> Dad.

> GEORGE
> (Startled)
> What?

> FRANK
> Cup of tea for you.

> GEORGE
> Oh. Thanks a million.

GEORGE sits up. He looks a bit wrecked.

> GEORGE
> Good man.

FRANK leaves. GEORGE sits with the tray on his lap. He just looks at the tray.

15.   EXT. COAST MORNING

JOE cycles to school. He sees a girl, TARA, standing at a bus stop. She is
JOE's age and wears a school uniform. She has short blonde hair. She is
chatting to a BOY. She smokes. JOE stares at her. She looks at him. He
looks away.

16.   INT. KITCHEN MORNING

RAY comes in to CARMEL, doing the dishes.

                          RAY
              Do you want a lift?

She comes to him and embraces him.

                          CARMEL
              Is that your best offer?

                          RAY
              I've got to give a lecture.

                          CARMEL
              Why don't you lecture me?

                          RAY
              Why don't you get your coat?

17.   EXT. COAST MORNING

JOE cycles along the seafront to school. He sees a boy of his age, DAMIEN,
loitering at the schoolgates, having a cigarette.

18.   INT. CLASSROOM MORNING

JOE's class. A classroom of sixteen-year-old boys. JOE sits alone. The
teacher, Mr FANNING, is young, well-built and speaks with a broad
country accent. He addresses the class while gazing out the window.

                          FANNING
              I don't like messers because I don't like
              messing. And the classic is the one
              smart fella that drags the other fellas
              that aren't so smart down with him,
              because he likes a mess. But I'm here
              to tell you, that I make it my mission to
              ensure the monkey-boys don't be
              encouraging the civilised fellas to
              come up for a swing in the branches.
              And that's my policy. Do you like my
              policy, Hennessy?

HENNESSY is a broad-shouldered boy who looks like he's been kept back a few years.

> HENNESSY
> Yes Sir.

> FANNING
> Yes Sir. You do in your barney like it
> Sir. Now, next thing.

The boy JOE saw smoking, DAMIEN, comes in.

> FANNING
> Ah . . . Who's this? The new boy . . .
> (Looking at roll) The late Damien
> Fitzgibbon. You see they've left you the
> best desk and everything. Right up at
> the front beside me.

DAMIEN sits. FANNING regards him.

> FANNING
> Are you a messer, boy?

DAMIEN just looks at him.

> In my classroom, you're innocent until
> proven guilty. And you will be proven
> guilty. [Now next thing. You have to
> elect a prefect. And if I had my way
> about this, you'd elect a nice sensible
> fella like Kevin McCormack there or Joe
> Beneventi there, the mafia man, ha?
> But I know yous won't, because that'd
> be too sensible for monkey-boys like
> you. Isn't that right, Hennessy?

③

> HENNESSY
> Yes Sir.

> FANNING
> Yes Sir. Okay, everybody take out a slip
> of paper and write down a name. We
> don't have all day, come on.

The boys do so.

> FANNING
> Come on. This isn't an exercise in
> time-wasting. It's not an experiment,
> Jesus, Lawless, don't write it on a flag,
> just a little slip of paper, God help us,
> the waste. Yep. Democracy in action.

14

JOE sees HENNESSY and the BOY beside him organise for the BOY to cough while HENNESSY spits on DAMIEN's back. DAMIEN registers what has happened but doesn't turn around.

> FANNING
> McCormack. Collect them. Come on.

McCORMACK collects the slips. Mr FANNING begins counting them.

> FANNING
> Ah, yeah. No surprises so far. All the
> monkeys. Oh, a spoiled vote. I didn't
> think the electorate was that
> sophisticated.

He holds up a slip of paper. It is a crude sexual drawing of a penis and a vagina. The boys laugh.

> FANNING
> I realise there's no point in trying to
> find who did this. But the shit always
> rises to the top. And I'm a patient man.
> I'll give you the election results
> tomorrow. Fun's over. Take out your
> books.

The boys do so. JOE regards DAMIEN.

19. INT. BUS DAY

FRANK sits upstairs on a bus. The only other passenger is a TEENAGE GIRL who holds a BABY. The BABY is screaming, that red-faced hysterical crying. The GIRL seems to ignore the baby. FRANK gets up and rings the bell for his stop. As he passes the GIRL he pauses.

> FRANK
> You know, I think there might be some-
> thing wrong with your baby, you know?

The GIRL looks at him, then looks away. FRANK looks away in exasperation and leaves.

20. INT. MANPOWER OFFICE DAY

FRANK sits opposite a CLERK.

> CLERK
> Okay . . . Mr Beneventi . . . Is that
> Italian?

> FRANK
> My Dad's from Italy.

15

CLERK
Oh right. You have your Leaving.

FRANK
Yeah. Just about.

CLERK
Any post-Leaving Cert courses?

FRANK
No.

CLERK
Okay. You went straight into the job
you have now?

FRANK
Em. No. I drove an ice-cream van for
two years.

CLERK
But you're working in the chipper now.

FRANK
Yeah.

CLERK
And that's your father's business.

FRANK
Yeah.

CLERK
Can I ask you what happened with the
ice-cream job?

FRANK
Em. My mum became ill. And I had to
help Dad. So he could go to see her.

CLERK
Okay.

FRANK
But em . . . She died four years ago.
But the way these things go . . .

CLERK
You're still there . . .

FRANK
Yeah.

CLERK
And . . . Would you . . . Are you looking
for something in the same line, or do
you want to do something different,
or . . .

FRANK
Em. I'm really just . . . something in
town or . . . something . . .

CLERK
You want to get out of the house.

FRANK
(Smiles)
Basically.]

21.   EXT. UNIVERSITY MORNING

RAY parks his car and takes his briefcase. As he walks across the car park
he sees a student, DEBORAH. She stands smoking with some FRIENDS.
He ducks down and runs behind a line of cars and into the college.

22.   INT. UNIVERSITY (PHILOSOPHY SEMINAR ROOM) MORNING

RAY enters a room with tables set in a square around the centre of the
room. Around these sit PHILOSOPHERS from RAY's department. A few
have copies of Konigsberg's book in front of them. They chat, waiting for
a staff meeting to begin. RAY is possibly the youngest member of staff
except for a young woman who sits opposite him, DR TRISH MEEHAN.
She regards RAY coldly. He gives her a shallow smile. She doesn't smile
back. Professor TONY REGAN, sixties, head of the department, comes in
and takes a prominent seat, shuffling some papers.

REGAN
Sorry I'm late. We'll get straight to
business. This meeting is to finalise
the details of Konigsberg's visit.
Obviously we're all very pleased to
have managed to, to, to, get him. It's
an honour . . . And, ehm, the first thing
we need is someone to meet him at the
airport. So ah . . . volunteers?

Six hands go up, including TRISH MEEHAN's. RAY doesn't volunteer. He
wears a look of slight disdain.

REGAN
Oh. Right. Six. . . . Great then, okay. No
go, I'm afraid Ray, on the questions.
He's not taking any questions.

17

RAY

What?

REGAN

He can't, or he's not, taking any
questions.

RAY

That's insane.

TRISH

I don't think he should have to answer
any questions. He's ninety years of age,
Ray. He'll be exhausted from his lectures.

RAY

You don't think that's a bit
undemocratic, Trish? Just listening
to someone banging on for hours,
and not being allowed to question it?
(To the room:) Not to mention the
importance of discussion to the
progress of ideas . . . blah blah.

REGAN

It's not our fault, Ray. I know how
much you were looking forward to this.
We all were. I'd love to see you grill
him. But it's his choice. So this is all
academic.

RAY stands up and throws his stuff into his briefcase.

RAY

Okay. Well I don't see the point of
continuing the pursuit of truth and
knowledge under these conditions.

REGAN

Ray. Come on.

TRISH

How noble . . .

REGAN

What are you doing?

RAY

Teaching today would make me sick.

TRISH

So you're taking the day off?

RAY pauses.

                              RAY
              Konigsberg is going down. And I'm the
              man that's going to do it.

                            REGAN
          Ray . . .

                            TRISH
              Do you realise how sad that sounds?

                              RAY
          I don't care.

RAY leaves. The PHILOSOPHERS sit there.

[23.   INT. SCHOOL CORRIDOR DAY   ③

The boys wait outside the Biology lab. HENNESSY and other boys mess at
the top of the stairwell. DAMIEN is jostled. JOE watches DAMIEN
surreptitiously push HENNESSY's schoolbag behind HENNESSY at the top
step. HENNESSY steps backwards and falls rather badly down the stairs.
The boys are shocked for a moment. HENNESSY groans and starts to get
up. The boys laugh. DAMIEN is impassive.

24.   INT. BIOLOGY LAB DAY

Miss BROSNAN, the biology teacher, is walking around. She is gorgeous
and has a fantastic figure. The boys have the microscopes out.

                            BROSNAN
              Come on. Stop messing. Pair up.

JOE goes to share a microscope. Two other boys are there already. They
are looking at a piece of snot.

                            BROSNAN
              Joe Beneventi up here, share with Damien.

She indicates where DAMIEN sits alone. JOE goes over. He nods at
DAMIEN. DAMIEN nods back.

                            BROSNAN
              Okay. For animal cells . . . Are you
              listening? For animal cells, scrape the
              inside, look, scrape the inside of your
              cheek with your nail. Do you see that?
              Make sure you've got clean hands.

Boys do it. DAMIEN watches Miss BROSNAN with her fingers in her
mouth. This is quite sexy. She has good lips.

                         BROSNAN
              And you'll be able to see those cells.
              Don't have it on high power to begin
              with. You won't see anything.

                           JOE
                        (To DAMIEN)
              Do you want to do it?

                         DAMIEN
              Nah, you do it.

JOE scrapes the inside of his cheek and spreads it on the slide. While he
tries to focus the microscope, DAMIEN just looks at Miss BROSNAN.

                           JOE
              Do you want to see?

DAMIEN glances down the microscope, but his attention is divided, mostly
between Miss BROSNAN's breasts and legs.

                         BROSNAN
              And I want you to make a sketch of
              what you see. I want membrane, and
              I want the nucleus.

DAMIEN twists the focus knob.

                         DAMIEN
              Sorry, Miss?

                         BROSNAN
              Yes, Damien?

                         DAMIEN
              I can't really see anything.

JOE looks at him quizzically. Miss BROSNAN comes over. She turns the
viewer around and has a look. She bends forward. DAMIEN takes full
advantage and peers down her top at her breasts.

                         BROSNAN
              You haven't even got it focused.

DAMIEN nudges JOE and urges him to look down her top. JOE hesitates
and then does so. He gets quite an eyeful for a boy his age. Miss
BROSNAN straightens up.

                         BROSNAN
              You can see them now.

She moves away. JOE and DAMIEN look at each other and laugh.

25.   EXT. STREET DAY

FRANK comes down the street with a newspaper, smoking a cigarette. He
watches a young woman painting a logo on the side of a truck: 'Simple
Simon McCurdie. Peat Briquettes to your door.' FRANK watches her work.

> FRANK
> Yo, Lisa.

> LISA
> Hi Frank.

> FRANK
> This not Tommy Dillon's truck?

> LISA
> Yeah, it was. It's Simple Simon's now.

> FRANK
> The whole business?

> LISA
> Tommy owed Simon a lot of money.

> FRANK
> Fucking hell.

He watches her work for a moment.

26.   EXT. CHIPPER BACKYARD DAY

GEORGE has his head under the car bonnet. FRANK comes out and gives
him a cup of tea.

> FRANK
> What are you doing?

> GEORGE
> Ha? Ah. Feels funny.

> FRANK
> What, it feels funny?

> GEORGE
> Mm. To drive. There's something . . .
> I'm having a look.

> FRANK
> You're having a look?

> GEORGE
> (Challenging)
> Yeah.

                              FRANK
            What do you think you're going to see?

                             GEORGE
            See what's wrong.

                              FRANK
            Yeah? See what's wrong with it?

                             GEORGE
            Yeah.

                              FRANK
            Well. You don't have to look under there.
            Just look at the fucking thing. It's old.
            It's banjacksed from being . . . an old
            car, like.

                             GEORGE
            Mm. How much do you think I'd . . .
            could get for it?

                              FRANK
            Ah now, here I think you're joking me
            are you?

                             GEORGE
            Ah, no. What do you think. I'm not
            looking for . . . I know it can't be much.

                              FRANK
            Yeah, well, you're right.

FRANK goes.

                              FRANK
                             (Leaving)
            'How much would I get for it!'

GEORGE considers the car. He takes a sup of tea.

                             GEORGE
                     (Absently. In to FRANK)
            That's a grand cup of tea.

                              FRANK
            Would you come in out of that?]

27.   INT. CHIPPER DAY

The first customers of the day have begun to come in for take-aways.
At the counter is one of the town's seemingly endless stream of old
drunks. FRANK has just served a BUILDER. The OLD MAN 'LARRY' doesn't

                                22

seem to want anything, he just stands there. FRANK stands on the other side of the counter, without needing to ask LARRY anything. They both look out at the sea. LARRY drinks a can of cider.

Outside a squad car pulls up driven by a uniformed garda. A female plainclothes detective, SGT DUGGAN, gets out and comes into the chipper.

LARRY
Here's the police.

DUGGAN
Larry . . . Hi Frank. Two snack boxes.

LARRY
Well Sergeant. Caught any criminals today?

DUGGAN
Fairly slow today, Larry. How's business with yourself?

LARRY
The business of generally getting so off my face I don't realise I'm going to my toilet in my trousers? Bit slow today as well, actually.

DUGGAN
Slow all round then.

LARRY
Wasn't slow for you when yous were chasing republicans all over the country. Only trying to make us a free socialist republic you treacherous bitch.

FRANK
Ah, here Larry, out.

FRANK comes around and puts LARRY out.

FRANK
Sorry about that, Sergeant.

DUGGAN
Why is everyone in this town always pissed, Frank.

FRANK continues working.

                    FRANK
No direction.

                    DUGGAN
Not like you. (She regards him for a
moment) You would think about the
Guards, Frank, no?

                    FRANK
I don't think I'd be brilliant at taking
orders in fairness now, Sergeant. You
know?

                    DUGGAN
We'd knock that out of you. Sure that's
what you do all day, anyway.

                    FRANK
What.

                    DUGGAN
Take orders.

                    FRANK
            (Smiles at her)
What are you trying to do to me here,
destroy my self-esteem or something?

                    DUGGAN
Trying to give you some.

DUGGAN becomes slightly awkward now and pretends to be interested in
a newspaper on the counter during the following:

                    DUGGAN
Oh here have you been in that new
place out in Lusk?

                    FRANK
Nah . . . I sort of stay local really.

                    DUGGAN
I was thinking I might go out some
night. Supposed to be fairly good. If
you . . . fancied it some night . . .

                    FRANK
            (Horrified)
Yeah . . . em . . . eh . . . But you know,
I might have to . . .

He indicates some vague obstacle behind him.

DUGGAN
Will you do me a favour, Frank?

FRANK
Yeah?

DUGGAN
Don't have a heart attack. And forget
I asked.

They are both mortified.

[28.   EXT. YARD DAY   ④

Little Break. JOE and DAMIEN stand together. DAMIEN is smoking. He
hands the cigarette to JOE. JOE takes a hesitant pull and starts coughing.

DAMIEN
Are you alright?

JOE
(Speaking with difficulty)
I have a cold.]

29.   INT. CLASSROOM DAY

Mr FANNING walks around the class, smoking his chalk. JOE and DAMIEN
sit together.

FANNING
Because it was one of the causes. However,
what phrase can I not stand, Duignan?

DUIGNAN
That 'the assassination was the match
which lit a steadily increasing pile of
tinder,' Sir.

FANNING
That's right, Sir. And why don't I like
that phrase, Beneventi?

JOE
Because it's in the book, Sir.

FANNING
Because it's in the book. And why do I
not like phrases in the book, Lawless?

LAWLESS
Because every eejit in the land will
write it in the exam Sir.

25

                    FANNING
          That's right. But about half of you will
          still write that. Won't yous, Logan.

                    LOGAN
          Yes Sir.

                    FANNING
          Yes Sir.

DAMIEN has been doodling. FANNING stops at his desk.

                    FANNING
          And what have we here, Sir?

FANNING picks up the doodle. It is another crude sexual depiction.

                    FANNING
          Didn't take long to find our artist. Did it
          Fitzer?

DAMIEN doesn't answer.

                    FANNING
          I said, did it, Fitzer?

                    DAMIEN
          No.

                    FANNING
          No Sir, or No Mr Fanning.

                    DAMIEN
          No Mr Fanny.

Some boys give a low nervous giggle.

                    FANNING
          What did you say?

                    DAMIEN
          No Sir.

                    FANNING
          Are you getting smart with me, boy?

                    DAMIEN
          No Sir.

                    FANNING
          Because I'd advise a little caution if
          this is the road you choose. Because
          you may be new, but I know your type.
          I've seen lots of you. Stand up.

                    26

DAMIEN rises. FANNING examines the picture.

> FANNING
> Is this how you see women? (Pause)
> Because I won't have this around me.
> And I certainly won't have it in one of
> my classes. Do you hear me? (Pause)

FANNING gives DAMIEN a vicious loud, thumping, deadener on the arm. DAMIEN knocks into JOE. DAMIEN leans forward clutching his arm.

> FANNING
> Do you hear me?

He grabs DAMIEN by the lock of hair in front of his ear and pulls him up by it. Agony.

> FANNING
> Do you hear me?

> DAMIEN
> Yeah.

> FANNING
> Yes what?

> DAMIEN
> Yes Sir.

> FANNING
> Sit down and don't let me catch you
> with this kind of filth again.

He throws the piece of paper into the bin and makes a little sound like an explosion. He smokes his chalk again.

> FANNING
> Ah yes. Give me another cause of the
> First World War, Rooney.

> ROONEY
> Imperialism, Sir.

> FANNING
> Could you not be a little bit more
> vague, Rooney, no?

JOE looks at DAMIEN. DAMIEN stares resolutely at the floor.

[30. INT. STUDENT BAR DAY   ⑤

RAY sits having a drink, reading his Konigsberg book. He sees DEBORAH, the student he seems to want to avoid, come in. He sneaks away.]

31.   INT. CHIPPER DAY

FRANK and GEORGE work behind the counter. SIMPLE SIMON and his nephew CHARLIE DUNNE come in and sit down in the table-service section. FRANK and GEORGE exchange a look. GEORGE goes out to deal with SIMON. SIMPLE SIMON is in his fifties, heavy set. He owns a lot of the town. CHARLIE is young and huge. FRANK watches his father being overly nice to SIMON. Another town drinker is at the counter, MACK. He swigs from a strange concoction in a plastic bottle.

> MACK
> Smoked cod and a large please Frank.

FRANK is distracted, watching GEORGE.

> MACK
> Yo! Frank Sinatra!

> FRANK
> Yeah, sorry. Smoked and a large.

> MACK
> I think you're thinking about the sexy
> ladies, are you?

> FRANK
> Yeah. I must be.

> MACK
> Yeah. You must be.

32.   INT. CHIPPER (SIT-DOWN PART) DAY

FRANK brings a plate piled with food over to CHARLIE and a pot of tea to SIMPLE SIMON. SIMPLE SIMON holds FRANK by the elbow, tenderly. CHARLIE immediately begins to eat ravenously.

> SIMON
> Ah. The Frank man. I think you do be
> avoiding me, do you?

> FRANK
> (Embarrassed)
> What?

> SIMON
> Ah, would you look at him! I'm only
> messing with you! You know Charlie,
> my nephew, don't you?

> FRANK
> How are you?

CHARLIE
(Mouth full)
How's it going?

SIMON
Charlie's doing a little bit of work for
me. Aren't you?

CHARLIE
Yeah . . .

SIMON winks at FRANK.

SIMON
How do you find it, son? Not the worst
job in the world . . .

CHARLIE
(Stuffing his face)
Yeah, it's great.

SIMON
A growing youth, ha? (To FRANK)
Come here to me, when are you going
to come down and see me?

SIMON flicks FRANK's apron.

SIMON
I'll give you a man's job. Proper wage.

FRANK
Yeah, you know, Mr McCurdie, I've got
to . . .

SIMON
Come here to me, sit down there.

SIMON guides FRANK to sit down beside him.

SIMON
Now. How are you?

FRANK
Yeah, I'm grand.

SIMON
Yeah? Because, come here. I do like to
have a few lads around the place.
Keeps the shit away from the bookies.
Get the van out. Deliver the briquettes.

FRANK

Yeah, it's my dad, Mr McCurdie, he
needs me here.

SIMON

I know how you feel, son, and I'm very
fond of your dad. But there's nothing
for a fella like you staying in this town.
You know? There really isn't. Eventually,
you put in a little bit of graft for me,
I can put you into any cybercafé in the
city centre, like that You know? You
should think about it.

FRANK

Yeah.

SIMON

Will you now, though?

FRANK

I will, yeah.

SIMON

Good man. Come here, get yourself a
drink.

SIMON tries to slip FRANK a tenner on the sly.

FRANK

Ah no. I couldn't.

SIMON

Ah, come on.

FRANK
(Gets up)
Ah no, really. I'm fine. It's fine.

SIMON

Okay. Won't you think about it, yeah?

FRANK

Yeah.

SIMON

Good man. I'll let you get back. Tell
your dad I'm off, will you? (To
CHARLIE:) Come on, finish that off, we
have to get going. Earn a few bob, ha?

SIMON is sort of nodding at people and talking to the room as he gets up.

                    SIMON
          This is it. Good man. Jaysus, what kind
          of a day is that, ha?

GEORGE comes out wiping his hands.

                    GEORGE
          Are yous away?

                    SIMON
          We're away George. Come here to me.

They shake hands.

                    SIMON.
          That's a grand youngfella you got
          there.

                    GEORGE
          Aw Jays. I know. I'd be lost without
          him.

                    SIMON
          I know you would. Fella like that's hard
          to find. I'm jealous of you. (With
          strange amusement) When are you
          coming down to me?

                    GEORGE
          Yeah. I'm sorry. I didn't get down
          before.

                    SIMON
          Ah yeah, no problem. But get down.
          Keep it steady. (A reassuring wink)
          Come on. Bye.

SIMON and CHARLIE leave. GEORGE gets back to work.

                    FRANK
          Don't be wiping your hands for that
          cunt.

                    GEORGE
          Ha?

FRANK won't answer.

33.   EXT. PLAYING FIELD DAY

JOE and DAMIEN sit near a small hillock. DAMIEN is smoking.

31

                    JOE
         How long have you been smoking?

                  DAMIEN
         Ah. Years.

                    JOE
         Yeah? Do you smoke at home?

                  DAMIEN
         Ah yeah.

                    JOE
         Do your folks not mind?

                  DAMIEN
         It's just me and my mum. And she
         couldn't give a fuck.

                    JOE
         What do you think of this school?

                  DAMIEN
         It's full of assholes.

                    JOE
         Why did you leave your last school?

                  DAMIEN
         Ah, being on the mitch. And I told a
         teacher to fuck off, and she was just
         out of hospital or something and she
         started crying. Like it was my fault.

DAMIEN sees something. Mr FANNING and another teacher are on the
playing field with hurling sticks. They bang a sliotar around.

                  DAMIEN
         Pair of fucking dicks.

                    JOE
         He can be alright sometimes.
         Sometimes he'll just spend the whole
         class reading us stuff out of the paper.
         And slagging it off, like.

JOE has a look. Mr FANNING is trying to reach up a tree with his hurl.
The other teacher comes over. They discuss it

                  DAMIEN
         They're after banging the ball up into
         the tree.

Mr FANNING bends down and the other teacher gets on his shoulders.

                    DAMIEN
          Don't tell me . . .

Mr FANNING stands up. The other TEACHER reaches into the tree with
the hurl. DAMIEN looks around and picks up a smooth stone.

                    JOE
          What are you doing?

                    DAMIEN
          Do you want to see a good aim?

                    JOE
          No.

                    DAMIEN
          Don't look then.

DAMIEN throws a high arcing shot which descends right onto the side of
Mr FANNING's head. Mr FANNING wobbles for a moment, trying to regain
his balance, but with the weight of the other TEACHER he finally sinks to
his knees. They both tumble to the ground.

                    DAMIEN
          Beautiful . . . We better get going.

                    JOE
          Fuck!

They get on their bikes.

34.   EXT. STREET DAY

JOE and DAMIEN cycle quickly down the road. DAMIEN is ecstatic. JOE's
terror turns to laughter.
                                                              ⑥
                   [DAMIEN
          We better split up. See you tomorrow.]

They part company.

35.   INT. CHIPPER DAY

JOE comes in. FRANK and GEORGE sit reading the paper, drinking tea. No
business.

                    FRANK
          Ah ha . . . The scholar.

                    GEORGE
          How was it?

33

> JOE
>
> Bit of doss, for a change.

> FRANK
>
> Do you want something to eat?

> JOE
>
> Yeah, alright.

> FRANK
>
> You okay?

FRANK works. JOE sits with GEORGE.

> JOE
>
> Yeah, I'm fine.

> FRANK
>
> I was thinking we might get up to the
> grave this weekend, yeah? Dad?

> GEORGE
>
> Yeah. If I can get the car in order.

> FRANK
> (Comic derision)
> Yeah right. Will we go up, Joe, yeah?

> JOE
>
> Whatever.

GEORGE regards JOE. JOE looks at him. GEORGE winks and knocks
softly on the table two or three times. A gesture of reassurance. (As if to
say 'chin up'.)

> TITLE BOARD: 'Tuesday'

36.   INT. CHIPPER DAY

FRANK comes into the back where GEORGE is counting money, mostly
pound coins.

> GEORGE
>
> Em. Have you got any money on you,
> son?

> FRANK
>
> Like how much?

> GEORGE
>
> Like say twelve, fifteen.

> FRANK
>
> What's it for?

GEORGE

Ah, it's for . . .

FRANK

Simple Simon?

GEORGE

I'm a tiny bit fucking short here. Come
on.

FRANK

Twelve quid short?

GEORGE

Ah, you know, I like to give him fifty.
(Short pause) At a time.

FRANK

How long are you going to be paying it
off?

GEORGE

Another three months'll see it.

FRANK.

It's been fucking years, but. How much
is it?

GEORGE

What?

FRANK

Overall. What, two grand?

GEORGE

Two and a half.

FRANK

What's wrong with the bank, man?

GEORGE

Ah, the bank.

FRANK
(Imitating GEORGE)
'The bank.' What? 'The bank'. We want
to get you down the bank, get a loan,
pay Simon off. You're not gonna be
crippled with this fucking shit.

GEORGE

Yeah, yeah, come on.

                    FRANK
What?

                    GEORGE
Just stop. You're giving me a fucking
headache. Alright?

                    FRANK
Alright. Cool the head. I'm giving it to
you. (Pause. Smiles:) What are you
like?

                    GEORGE
                    (Smiles)
I don't know.

                    FRANK
You're a fucking header.

                    GEORGE
I know.

                    FRANK
                    (Counting money)
You know, fucking, say it to him. We're
out of season. It's a killer. Ask him.
Give us a break. Just till summer kicks
in. It's fucking shit now.

                    GEORGE
Yeah.

                    FRANK
Will you say it to him?

                    GEORGE
I said yeah.

                    FRANK
Go on out of that you bollocks.
I'm gonna come down with you.

                    GEORGE
I will! I fuck . . . I'm going to.
[Givus that bottle.   ⑦

FRANK passes GEORGE a bottle of whiskey from a press.

                    FRANK
Your bottle! You're like a baby.

GEORGE goes to pour himself a drink.

                           FRANK
              I'll pour it. You giving yourself a pint of
              whiskey. I don't know what you're like.

GEORGE smiles. FRANK watches him take a drink.]

                           FRANK
              You're a knacker. Get your coat on. I'm
              coming down with you.

                           GEORGE
              Look at you. You're like an old man.
              When are you going to act yourself out
              of this shithole?

37.   INT. SIMPLE SIMON'S BOOKIES DAY   ⑧

GEORGE and FRANK come in. A few PUNTERS fill in dockets, stand
around smoking etc. One or two punters acknowledge GEORGE. CHARLIE
sits on a stool watching a race. They approach the clerk, ORLA, who
jadedly leafs through a paper.

                           GEORGE
              Hiya Orla. Is he in?

                           ORLA
              Yah, he's in the back. D'you want to
              come round? I'm not going.

                           GEORGE
              Thanks a million.

38.   INT. BOOKIES OFFICE DAY

ORLA leads them into the Office. SIMON is on the phone. He waves
them in.

GEORGE and FRANK come in and sit down. ORLA shuts the door. While
they wait for SIMON to finish his conversation, FRANK takes in the room.
Photos of SIMON posing with politicians and jockeys. There is a calendar
with a topless lady.
                                                                   ⑨
                          [SIMON
                        (On phone)
              No, it was. It was, a great night. I did.
              Big magnum. We'll be drinking it 'til
              Christmas, I tell you. There's eating and
              drinking in it. Mostly drinking. No, it
              was great. I did. I sponsored the last
              race. Did I fuck! The only thing I won
              was a spot prize, ha? And we all got

                             37

dirty calendars. Oh, typical. In April
I know! But I had the Hogan fella. bend-
ing the ear off me last night. All this,
that he has to walk four miles to work.
And a dog bit the arse out of him Thursday morning. Sure, what does he want
me to do? I said it to him. 'You should
have thought of that, you never thought
of that and you playing cards ten nights
in a row down in the back of Reynold's
pub.' I told his mother last November I
had to bar him out of this place. He
hadn't a shilling. What use is an Opel
Vectra to me? And it sitting out in the
shed. I have the keys here in a drawer.
Oh Charlie. Oh yeah. Listen, I'll do that
for you. I'll see you on Friday. Yeah. Good
man. Bye. Bye. (Hangs up) George, my
man. Frank, (Indicates calendar) do you
like my girlfriend? I saw you admiring
her. Would you like to look at that? What
the hell are they like? Ha?

GEORGE

Very nice.

SIMON

Very nice is right! That's what we want.
Calendar girls. A different lady every
month. I wouldn't say Frank here is
ever too short of the old offers, ha?

GEORGE
(Nodding)
Oh yeah . . . He's eh . . .

SIMON

On the lookout.

GEORGE

Looking after us, I think, is more like it.

SIMON

I know. I know. Yeah. He's great. Look
at him sitting there, All embarrassed.

They laugh.

SIMON

Am I giving you a hard time? Will I shut
up? I think I better, ha?

38

They laugh.]

> SIMON
>
> What can I do for you?

GEORGE proffers money.

> GEORGE
>
> Just to . . .

> SIMON
>
> Oh good man. What's here?

> GEORGE
>
> Should be fifty.

> SIMON
>
> (Going to safe)
> I trust you, George, Jaysus, at this
> stage.

SIMON opens the safe and puts the money in a little box. He then selects one of many ledgers and takes it to the desk.

> SIMON
>
> (To calendar)
> Now. What is it today, darling? The
> fourth . . .

SIMON writes in the ledger. FRANK nudges GEORGE.

> GEORGE
>
> Could you give us an idea how we
> stand, Simon, at the moment?

> SIMON
>
> Of course I can. Now . . .

SIMON begins to read the ledger. He stops abruptly.

> SIMON
>
> Is everything alright?

> GEORGE
>
> Yeah just so I know where we are.

> SIMON
>
> No, you're right. Don't ever apologise.
> Now. Initially, you borrowed two, yeah?

> GEORGE
>
> Two two.

SIMON

Sorry. Two two. And a subsequent five
hundred.

GEORGE

. . . Five hundred . . .

SIMON

That's right. And you want . . .

GEORGE

Just to know where we are.

ORLA enters with a tray of cups and a teapot. She puts it on the desk.
FRANK and GEORGE move out of her way. She leaves.

SIMON

So that was two two. Two thousand two
hundred and then the five. That's two
seven. Right?

GEORGE

Okay.

SIMON

Thanks Orla. And we said . . . What
did we say? I said, what, twelve
months before you . . . before you had
to give me anything. Okay? (To
FRANK:) Jays, he's a terrible fella. And
we said then, ten? . . . Per cent? Per
year we deal?

GEORGE

Yeah . . .

SIMON

Okay. So let me do this. Two seven.
Ten per cent is two seventy, by two,
five forty. On to two seven is . . . thirty-
two forty.

Simon indicates tea.

Frank, will you do the honours there,
like a good man.

Frank pours.

Now you have given me, in the last two
years . . . one two three four five six
seven eight nine ten eleven twelve,
da da da da forty, forty-four payments

40

of fifty pounds, no, including this
forty five, I'm writing that in now.
Which is . . . Is there no milk? Here,
hang on.

He gets milk from the table.

Two thousand and fifty. Take that from
thirty-two two-forty, is one thousand
one hundred and ninety pounds.
Outstanding. Okay?

                    GEORGE
Mm hm.

                    SIMON
Alright?

SIMON closes the ledger. FRANK nudges GEORGE.

                    GEORGE
I'm em, I don't really want to slip into
another year at ten per cent Simon.
To be honest with you.

                    SIMON
Okay. You want to get it out of the way.

                    GEORGE
Yeah, but I don't think I have the one . . .

                    SIMON
One one nine o.

                    GEORGE
Yeah. In one block. If we could . . . (A
cheesy little laugh) If we could wait until
things are back in season. It'd make it a
lot easier for me, you know yourself. I
rely on my few regulars. I'm kind of
ticking over until the summer. And I just
know I'm going to slip into another year
at ten per cent I just know I am.

                    SIMON
So you want to take a break, in the
payment.

                    GEORGE
Well, yeah. But we could leave it that
it's not part of this year. We hold it at
this year's ten per cent. The twenty
in all.

41

SIMON

That might seem like the thing to do.
But I don't recommend it. These things
are better . . . when when you keep it
even, keep it steady. Nice, bam, bam,
bam. You take a break, you see, you
don't budget for it. You find the
money's going into something else.
You're in a routine. Come time to pay
again, you're back in the same
situation. You're looking for the fifty.
Believe me.

GEORGE

Mmm.

SIMON

Mmm. And I've seen it too many times
to let that happen to you. (Short pause)
George. You stuck?

GEORGE

Well . . .

SIMON

Mmm. Okay look. If you're . . . You
keep accounts down at the chipper?

GEORGE

Well. Basic. You know . . .

SIMON

Okay. You let me have a look. I'll see
what I can do. To speed it up. I might
come in. Float a little bit of money.
Maybe a grand. Fuck it. Maybe what
we have outstanding. We'll call that my
share. Be partners for six months. And
I get what you owe me out of the way
at the source. As partners. Then I'll
back out. And we'll be even. What do
you think of that? (Pause) Have a little
think.

39.   INT. CHIPPER DAY

FRANK and GEORGE come in. The chipper is closed.

FRANK

No fucking way.

                    GEORGE
Well, as far as I see it, it's that or this
for years.

                    FRANK
What were you thinking?

                    [GEORGE
He . . . let me off a bet. One Christmas.
I don't know.

                    FRANK
He let you off a bet?! What was it?
Three quid? A fiver?

                    GEORGE
It . . . was around that time. And I just
felt . . . ah fucking . . . I thought I had a
policy.

                    FRANK
What?

                    GEORGE
When Mammy went into hospital.
I thought I had a policy. But then when
she was that sick . . . we were all
upset. I forgot to pay it! Simon was
just the first thing came in my head.
I didn't know where to go. He was in
my mind after giving back that bet.
I'll deal with it!

GEORGE leaves.] FRANK stands there.

He picks up a bottle of ketchup and flings it at the wall.

40.   INT. LECTURE HALL DAY

RAY is lecturing his students.

                    RAY
[So let's respect nature for a moment.
Let's go down that road. If everything
has a purpose, the eye for seeing,
appetite for . . . survival, what role
could reason possibly have? To make
us happy? Maybe, but surely our
instincts are better at getting us what
we want It's not reason that tells us

                    43

when to eat or sleep. Also with our
sexual appetite . . .

Here, RAY makes eye-contact with DEBORAH.

> RAY
> Were we to be always reasonable, we
> may never get to bed!

The students laugh.

> RAY
> No. What reason governs is our will.
> Reason stops us merely doing what we
> want, when we want. It's the moment
> of reflection. The moment of pause in
> the moment of passion. The moment
> we could say, of humanity. Okay.]
> Time's up, but before we go, please
> don't forget that the famous, eminent
> philosopher, Professor Wolfgang
> Konigsberg, is visiting the college for
> three days from Wednesday. To
> expound his theory that language is
> dying. This is a rare opportunity for
> you to see an historical figure in
> philosophy while he's still alive. For
> the moment at least. People! Next time!

RAY watches DEBORAH get her stuff together for a moment.

41.   SHOT OF EMPTY CORRIDOR

41A.   INT. RAY'S OFFICE DAY   ⑫

RAY is in his office. There's a knock at the door. RAY seems hesitant
There's another knock.

> RAY
> It's open.

DEBORAH comes in. They start laughing.

> DEBORAH
> Hi . . .

> RAY
> Sit down. Look love. I've been thinking
> about this. And . . . I can't. I'm . . . with
> somebody.

DEBORAH

Oh. Oh right. Okay.

RAY

And I can't hurt them.

DEBORAH

Maybe you should have said
something.

RAY

I know. I know. But regardless. This is
a professional fucking thing I could
lose my job over.

DEBORAH

Okay. Okay. I know that. But it's like . .
. I don't want this to become a thing
where I feel like, 'Oh, Okay.' And like
you gave me a line. And I went for it.

RAY

I don't think I did. I said some stuff but
that's because I get too intense about
this fucking shit. And it's like, we both
said, it's not like it came out of
nowhere. Like that time when you
brought back the book.

DEBORAH

I know. But now you're saying it's
nothing?

RAY

I'm not. What have I . . . what have I just
said? I haven't felt like this since I was
a teenager. Well you are a teenager.

DEBORAH

Ray, I'm twenty-one.

RAY

Oh. 'Twenty-one', sorry.

DEBORAH

Don't be so sarcastic.

RAY

I'm not being sarcastic. I'm sorry. I feel
awful.

                    DEBORAH
        I woke up this morning, I felt sick.
        I haven't eaten anything in two days.

RAY looks at her fearfully.

                    DEBORAH
        No . . . I'm not!

They laugh.

                    RAY
        For fuck's sake, Deborah.

                    DEBORAH
        You should see your face.

                    RAY
        Jesus, for a minute, I fucking . . .

                    DEBORAH
        What are we like?

                    RAY
        I know.

                    DEBORAH
        So, that's it . . .

                    RAY
                (Exasperated)
        I don't know.

                    DEBORAH
        Look. Do you want me to just go?

                    RAY
        Well, I know you should go, yeah.

                    DEBORAH
        Yeah, but do you want me to?

                    RAY
        No. I don't think I do.

CUT TO EXT. CORRIDOR VIEW OF RAY'S OFFICE – FIGURES CROSS THE
FOREGROUND.

[42. INT. DESERTED AMUSEMENT ARCADE EVENING   ⑬

JOE plays a rifle game. SIMPLE SIMON is at the cash desk. JOE doesn't
really pay any attention.

                    SIMON
          Is he in? He's not in? Oh, he is in?
          (Pause) Is he around? (Laughter) If you
          don't mind.

     SIMON looks around, sees JOE, turns his attention back to the desk.]

43.   INT. BATHROOM NIGHT

     FRANK shaves meticulously. He looks at himself as though testing
     somebody's mettle.

44.   INT. REYNOLD'S BAR NIGHT

     FRANK sits having a pint, listening to two town drinkers, MACK and
     LARRY. They chat to the barman, TEDDY.

                    MACK
          She was the most beautiful girl, you
          know?

                    LARRY
          Oh Jesus, yes.

                    MACK
          She was something in this town.
          Something to behold.

                    LARRY
          We used to be down there in the
          courtyard on our break, Tim. Fuck me.
          We'd be having our . . . sandwiches.
          How many of us would there be?

                    MACK
          Ten or twelve anyway. Oh yeah. And
          she'd come down the, she'd come
          down the fucking road, in the summer.
          Wheeling her bike.

                    LARRY
          The little sandals on her.

                    MACK
          Her brown legs like a pair of fucking . . .
          what you'd have in the best, places, in
          the world.

                    LARRY
          She'd break your fucking heart!

BARMAN

Yous never spoke to her.

MACK

No! You wouldn't!

LARRY

Sure, what would you fucking say, man?
That was that and that was what it was.

MACK

It's not for us. It's not for you. That's
what was the way we thought about it.

LARRY

But Jesus fucking Christ! To see her
now? The big fat lump she is. You'd
nearly shit yourself, she's that ugly.

MACK

It'd break your heart.

A young man, JOHN TRAYNOR, comes in. He is thin and muscular, very
short hair. A fantastic scar down one side of his face. He moves restlessly,
always dancing a little bit. He is Frank's age. A bit pissed. FRANK sits in a
corner unnoticed. He watches JOHN carefully.

MACK

Oh now. Jaysus.

LARRY

How are you doing, son?

MACK

What'll you have?

JOHN

Ah no, lads, I'll look after myself.

MACK

Ah no. We'll get you one.

JOHN

Ah no, I'll look after myself. Pint of
cider please, Teddy.

LARRY

How are you doing?

JOHN

Doing good.

LARRY

You're on the right track.

                    JOHN
        Ah yeah.

                    LARRY
        Yeah?

                    JOHN
        Yeah. Don't fuck me up here boys.

                    MACK
        Ahh. Yeap. Anybody, I think, can be led
        astray.

                    LARRY
        Now you said it.

                    MACK
        He was always a good boy in here.
        (Indicates his heart) Where it counts.

JOHN takes his pint.

                    JOHN
        Okay. I'm going to skull this and then I
        need to sort of fly into the night so . . .

He raises his glass.

                    MACK
        Oh yeah. And enjoy the, the pint, your
        drink, and the atmosphere, and your,
        your liberty. And cheers. Cheers.

JOHN drains his drink. FRANK continues to watch him from his corner.
JOHN puts down his glass, hitches his trousers up awkwardly and leaves.
THE OLD MEN nod and smile at him.

                    MACK
        There goes one of the maddest fucking
        headbangers this town ever produced.

                    LARRY
        A fucking mentler.

FRANK considers them and leaves.

45.   EXT. STREET NIGHT

FRANK jogs down the street. He sees JOHN TRAYNOR finish urinating
against a wall. FRANK approaches him.

                    FRANK
        Yo, eh, John, man, how's it going?

49

                         JOHN
     Ah Frank! Yeah.

                         FRANK
     You okay?

                         JOHN
     Yeah. Wrecked, you know, got out
     Monday. I've just done this thing where
     I'm having a pint in every pub in town.
     That's nine pints you know?

                         FRANK
     That's eh . . . that's good going, yeah.

                         JOHN
     Yeah, it is good going, when you stop
     to consider that all the pubs are full of
     all old smelly bastards.

                         FRANK
     Yeah . . .

They stand there. FRANK is obviously trying to work up the nerve to ask
JOHN something.

                         JOHN
         What's up?

FRANK looks nervously at JOHN.

46.   EXT. JOHN'S BACK SHED NIGHT

     JOHN leads FRANK in. They look suitably shifty. Collars up. JOHN hits the
     light a second too late. FRANK falls over a bike.

                         JOHN
         Watch the fucking bike, man, will you?

                         FRANK
         It was right in the fucking doorway,
         here.

     JOHN begins to look around the shed, picking bits and pieces up.

                         JOHN
         Yeah, yeah, everyone's judge and jury.

46A.   INT. JOHN'S BACK SHED NIGHT

     FRANK watches while JOHN works. He takes a length of copper pipe and
     saws it in half. He tapes the two lengths together and finds a can of black

spray-paint He sprays the pipes. He puts one end in his coat, sticking the other end out like a double-barrelled shotgun. He makes a machine-gun sound.

> JOHN
> That do you?

He hands it to FRANK. FRANK gets the feel of it.

47.   INT. LANDING EVENING

JOE comes down the landing to GEORGE's bedroom. CARMEL is sorting a woman's clothes into bags.

> CARMEL
> Hi.

> JOE
> Hi.

CARMEL continues to work. JOE watches all his mother's stuff in her hands. He looks at a photograph of his mother which is on the bedside table.

> CARMEL
> Stupid. All this stuff still lying here.

> JOE
> Yeah.

He continues to watch her.

[48.   INT. BEDROOM NIGHT   ⑭

FRANK and JOE are in bed. JOE begins to have a sneaky wank.

> FRANK
> I can hear you doing that.

> JOE
> (Startled. Still)
> What?

> FRANK
> I can hear you doing that.

> JOE
> I'm not doing anything.

> FRANK
> I don't really give a fuck, man. That's
> cool. Just do it in the jacks. Alright?

51

JOE

I'm not doing anything, but.

FRANK

Okay, fine. Forget about it.

They lie there. Finally, JOE gets up and leaves for the bathroom.

49.   INT. GEORGE'S BEDROOM NIGHT

GEORGE leans out of bed and pours a little nip of whiskey.

50.   INT. CARMEL'S ROOM NIGHT

CARMEL reads. She puts the book down and turns the light out.

51.   INT. DEBORAH'S BEDROOM NIGHT

RAY and DEBORAH sadly have very little self-restraint. This isn't a 'moment of pause.']

TITLE BOARD: 'Wednesday'

52.   JOE'S DREAM – THE PAST

We see a few seconds of Joe's dream. The sound bleeds out. The vivid colours. The home-movie feel. The woman on the beach.

53.   INT. BEDROOM MORNING

Sound bleeds in. Joe's eyes open.

54.   EXT. COAST MORNING

JOE cycles to school. Again he sees TARA standing at the bus stop. She is smoking. He stares at her. She sees him. He looks away.

55.   INT. SCHOOL HALL MORNING

THE HEADMISTRESS has the school assembled. Sitting near her is SGT DUGGAN, the female plainclothes detective. She watches the boys carefully, calmly. The HEADMISTRESS addresses the boys.

HEAD

This is very simple. On Monday
afternoon, Mr Fanning was struck on
the head with a stone.

JOE looks over at DAMIEN. DAMIEN doesn't react.

HEAD

And Mr Gibney was also injured. He was lucky and only has a sprained wrist. However, Mr Fanning was unconscious for about thirty seconds, which is very serious. And he has been kept in hospital for observation. Now this is the way that I see it. Some boy knows who has done this, if only the boy himself. And I am going to find out who it was. Because this boy decided to inflict suffering on others. Well I'm going to give that boy a feast. He can inflict suffering on the whole school. Until he comes forward, or is brought forward, the whole school will be detained each Wednesday and Thursday, starting today.

The BOYS groan.

You see, boys, This is not simply a school matter. It's a matter for the guards. This is Sergeant Duggan and she is very concerned to find out who did this, and to see that they are brought to book for what we all consider to be a very serious incident.

JOE looks at SGT DUGGAN. She looks at him.

56.   EXT. SCHOOLYARD DAY

Little break. JOE and DAMIEN stand in the bike shed. DAMIEN is smoking.

JOE

What are you going to do?

DAMIEN

Well, I'm not going to do fucking detention.

JOE

The whole school's going to be in it.

DAMIEN

I'm not.

JOE

They'll make you go, man.

                    DAMIEN

Can't make me go if I'm not in school.
I'm bonking off this afternoon. And you
should as well.

                      JOE

Why?

                    DAMIEN

There's no point in you being in
detention for something I did. I'm an
expert forger. I'll give you a brilliant
note. What? Are you gonna rat on me?

                      JOE

No.

                    DAMIEN

Well then you're in it. I'll see you at the
roundabout. Two o'clock.

They stand there.

[57.   INT. DEBORAH'S BEDROOM MORNING   ⑮

RAY wakes up. He is in bed with DEBORAH. He is disorientated. He looks
at DEBORAH and very gingerly gets out of bed, so as not to wake her. He
is naked. He knocks over some empty bottles. He stops the noise quickly.
DEBORAH stirs, but doesn't wake. He looks at one of the bottles, some
stupid liqueur. He feels his head. He dresses with care and creeps out of
the room.

58.   SCENE DELETED

59.   SCENE DELETED

60.   EXT. COLLEGE DAY

RAY pulls into the car park.

61.   INT. RAY'S CAR DAY

RAY opens his glove compartment. He takes out a box of aspirin. It is
empty. He sighs heavily. He looks at the student bar. He looks at his watch.

62.   INT. STUDENT BAR DAY

RAY stands at the bar. It isn't busy yet. A student works behind the bar,
cleaning, etc.

RAY
How are you doing? Come here to me.
What's good for a really bad hangover?

BARMAN
Sleep.

RAY
Yeah. No. I mean for a cure.

BARMAN
(Looks at bottles)
I'm not really sure. Port or something,
isn't it?

RAY
Gin and tonic, is it? Is that supposed to
do it?

BARMAN
Yeah, well the tonic is probably
medicinal. I mean, I'd imagine.

RAY
Are you a medical student?

BARMAN
No, sorry man. Agriculture.

RAY
Agriculture, yeah?

BARMAN
Yeah.

RAY
But you'd have an idea about
chemicals and so on.

BARMAN
Yeah, in fertiliser.

RAY
So the gin and tonic thing could well
be bullshit?

BARMAN
Well, yeah, that could well be a load of
fucking nonsense you know?

RAY
Okay. Give us a large gin and tonic.

63.   INT. STUDENT BAR LAVATORY MORNING

RAY gets sick. He washes his face and sees vomit on his shirt. He checks his watch.

                              RAY
            Oh . . . fuck.]

64.   EXT. DAMIEN'S HOUSE DAY

This is a large house. There is a boat in the driveway. JOE and DAMIEN arrive.

                              JOE
            Is that your boat?

                            DAMIEN
            Yeah. It doesn't go.

65.   INT. DAMIEN'S HOUSE DAY

DAMIEN leads JOE through the house.

                            DAMIEN
            Yo! Mum! She's not here.

The house is a bit rundown. Messy.

66.   INT. KITCHEN DAY

DAMIEN drifts around the kitchen. There's nothing to eat. He finds some bread and bangs it on the work-top.

                            DAMIEN
            Do you want some toast?

                              JOE
            Yeah, alright.

DAMIEN prepares some toast. JOE notices lots of empty bottles around the place.

                             [JOE
            Where's your dad?

                            DAMIEN
            He lives in England.

                              JOE
            Do you ever see him?

                            DAMIEN
            Nah. He's much older than my mum.

JOE looks out the back garden. It is large, overgrown. There is a muddy pond.

                    JOE
         Big garden.

                    DAMIEN
         Yeah.

[They hear the front door open. A huge dog runs straight into the   ⑯
kitchen. JOE gets a fright. The dog goes out the back. A MAN comes
through and follows the dog out the back. He is tanned, well-dressed.

                    MAN
         Hello men.

                    JOE
         Hello.

JOE watches as the MAN takes off his shirt and get into the pond with the dog.

                    JOE
         Who's that?

                    DAMIEN
         Don't know. Must know my mum.
         Mum?

DAMIEN looks out the door. His mother, Mrs FITZGIBBON, comes in,
carrying some shopping. She is in her thirties, attractive.

                    MRS FITZGIBBON
         What are you doing home?

                    DAMIEN
         They let us off early.

                    MRS FITZGIBBON
         Why?

                    DAMIEN
         Teachers' strike or something.

                    MRS FITZGIBBON
         I don't believe you.

She starts to put messages away.

                    DAMIEN
         Ask him.

                    MRS FITZGIBBON
         I'm not asking anyone. You have to
         stay in school. You're giving me such a
         hard time.

DAMIEN

Yeah, well, you're doing my fucking
head in. You should just believe me.

MRS FITZGIBBON

Why should I 'just believe you?'

DAMIEN

Because you're . . .

MRS FITZGIBBON

Why? What is that?

DAMIEN

Because you're, no, you're fucking up
my confidence and shit. It's like I don't
expect for people to think that I'm
telling the truth.

MRS FITZGIBBON

Okay. It's not worth it. Just leave it.
I don't care.

DAMIEN

Yeah. Now you're saying leave it.
Because you've got what you want out
of it, that like, I'm beneath you.

MRS FITZGIBBON

No I'm not, I'm just not getting into it.

DAMIEN

No, but you see, you shouldn't do that.

MRS FITZGIBBON

I'm not getting into it.

DAMIEN

Why, though?

MRS FITZGIBBON

Because you're horrible.

DAMIEN

Oh yeah, that's great . . .

MRS FITZGIBBON

You're burning your toast and
everything. Look at you.

DAMIEN

Ah . . . Fuck!

DAMIEN flings the toast out the back. It hits the dog.

MAN
Hey! Cool it! Go easy on the fucking
dog, people!

DAMIEN
Who the fuck is that?

MRS FITZGIBBON
That's Peter. He's a friend of mine.

PETER is putting his head under the water and coming up.

DAMIEN
Are you alright out there? Are you?

PETER
Yeah. Don't mind me. I'm a bit pissed.

DAMIEN
Yeah, cool. He's 'cool' Mum.

Pause.

MRS FITZGIBBON
Come here.

She embraces DAMIEN.

MRS FITZGIBBON
Don't fight with me. I don't like it.

DAMIEN
You're just such a fucking bitch, man,
you know?

MRS FITZGIBBON
I'm sorry.

She gives him a kiss. He puts his hand on her arse. She looks at JOE for
the first time.

MRS FITZGIBBON
Don't be doing that. You dirty knacker.

She goes out the back.

MRS FITZGIBBON
Peter. What are you doing?

DAMIEN
I'm sorry about that, man. She can be a
real painus in the anus.

JOE
Ehm. I think I'll head actually.]

[67.   EXT. FRONT GARDEN DAY

JOE gets on his bike.

> DAMIEN
> D'you not want to stick around, watch a
> video or something?

> JOE
> Nah, I got to get back. Help my dad.

> DAMIEN
> D'you want to go to Shadows tonight?

> JOE
> What is it?

> DAMIEN
> Nightclub. Behind the Ancient Mariner.
> Full of fit girls.

> JOE
> Ah, I've no ID.

> DAMIEN
> They don't look for ID. They don't
> refuse anybody.

> JOE
> I'll see. I don't know if I can.

> DAMIEN
> Tch. Come on. You know you're gonna
> go.]

68.   INT. FRANK AND JOE's ROOM DAY

> FRANK looks through the wardrobe. He
> finds a bobble hat. He sits on the bed
> and takes a scissors. He cuts eye-holes
> in the hat He pulls it on over his face
> and looks at himself in the mirror. He
> cuts the bobble off. He takes the
> 'shotgun' and points it around a bit.
> Tries different ways of holding it.

> FRANK
> Everybody on the fucking floor. Nobody
> fucking move. I'll blow your fucking
> heads off.

>   CARMEL
>   (From outside)
>   Frank?

FRANK throws himself against the door.

>   FRANK
>   Hold on.

He takes off the hat.

>   CARMEL
>   What are you doing?

He kicks the 'gun' under the bed.

>   FRANK
>   I'm moving the bed around.

>   CARMEL
>   You're moving the bed?

>   FRANK
>   Yeah, it's okay, come in.

He sits on the bed.

>   CARMEL
>   Are you alright?

>   FRANK
>   Yeah, grand. You home early?

>   CARMEL
>   No. Who were you talking to?

>   PRANK
>   Nah. It was the radio.

>   CARMEL
>   What radio?

>   FRANK
>   Is it not on downstairs, no?

>   CARMEL
>   I don't know.

FRANK nods at her in some sort of bizarre 'agreement'.

>   CARMEL
>   Frank?

>   FRANK
>   Yeah?

61

CARMEL
So you're having a bit of a play, are
you? In your room.

FRANK
You know, yourself . . .

CARMEL
I'll see you later.

FRANK
Okay.

CARMEL leaves. FRANK lies back on the bed with relief and
embarrassment.

[69.   EXT. BEACH LATE AFTERNOON   ⑲

A YOUNG WOMAN sits on the sand watching her child, a TODDLER,
playing. She, looks at the child like she knows it's for life, and she doesn't
like it. This the woman from Scene 19. At the edge of the frame we see
LARRY, the drunk, drop a can into the sea. He stoops to retrieve it and falls
in the water.]

[70.   INT. BATHROOM EVENING   ⑳

JOE puts aftershave on. Then he puts loads more on.]

71.   INT. REYNOLDS BAR NIGHT   ㉑

RAY and CARMEL sit in the bar. RAY is nervous and preoccupied. He
lowers a large drink.

CARMEL
Are you alright?

RAY
Eh . . . I don't treat you very well.

CARMEL
What are you talking about.

RAY
I know I don't. In the way I think about
you.

CARMEL
What way do you think about me?

RAY
I don't think about you enough.

                              CARMEL
                I think you're just being silly, are you?

                              RAY
                No. I'm sorry.

                              CARMEL
                I don't know what you have to be sorry
                about.

                              RAY
                I know you don't.

                              CARMEL
                Are you trying to confess something to
                me?

                              RAY
                I'm not that sorry.

They laugh. Pause.

72.   EXT. SHADOWS NIGHTCLUB NIGHT

YOUNG PEOPLE are queuing. JOE and DAMIEN are there. The BOUNCERS
are very strict. They turn a group of OLDER TEENAGERS away. A fight
breaks out. The BOUNCERS mill the OLDER TEENAGERS. The TEENAGERS
run away with shouts of 'You're fucking dead.' Etc. The queue disperses
while the fight happens. People scatter everywhere. The queue forms
again. The BOUNCERS continue to work as though nothing has happened.
JOE looks horrified.

                              DAMIEN
                It's good once you get in.

73.   INT. NIGHTCLUB FOYER NIGHT

DAMIEN and JOE are being searched. They move to a table where a
makeshift box office is in operation.

                              JOE
                How much is it?

                              BOUNCER 1
                Six pound.

                              JOE
                Six?

                              BOUNCER 1
                What am I after saying? Six.

                                63

BOUNCER 2
Come on! Move it on!

JOE pays.

BOUNCER 1
Put your coat in over there.

JOE
Can I not hang on to it, no?

BOUNCER 1
No you have to put it in. It's a pound.

[74.   INT. SHADOWS NIGHT   ㉒

The nightclub is packed. The music is monotonous techno. Very loud.
JOE, looking for DAMIEN, bumps into someone.

JOE
Sorry.

He sees DAMIEN talking to a GIRL. He goes to him.

JOE.
Alright?

DAMIEN nods. They all stand there.

JOE
(Shouts)
Do you want a drink?

DAMIEN puts his ear to JOE's mouth.

JOE
(Shouts)
Do you want a drink?

DAMIEN gives him a thumbs up. JOE makes his way to the bar.]

75.   INT. SHADOWS NIGHT

JOE waits for his drinks at the bar. He sees an OLDER TEENAGER, a boy,
kiss two girls in succession. JOE gets two pints. He looks for DAMIEN. He
sees him dancing. He tries to carry the drinks on to the dance floor. He is
jostled by the crowd. [BOUNCER 3 grabs him.   ㉓

BOUNCER 3
Where are you going?

JOE
I'm giving my mate his drink.

BOUNCER 3

There's no drinks on the dance floor.
Come on, back.

He pushes JOE back into the bar area. JOE stands with the two pints,
drinking from one of them.] TARA, the girl JOE sees at the bus stop, tugs
at his sleeve. He turns and they stare at each other for a moment. She is
very drunk, on the verge of tears. He's a bit wide-eyed and embarrassed.

TARA

Someone's after taking my bag.

JOE

(Pause)
Eh. Did you tell the bouncer?

TARA

I have to wait till the end.

JOE

Where did you have it?

TARA

I don't know.

JOE

You don't know where you left it, no?

TARA

I don't know where it is.

JOE

Do you want to ask at the cloakroom
did someone leave it in?

TARA

Will you ask?

JOE

Okay.

[TARA

What's your name?

JOE

Joe Beneventi.]

TARA

Thanks Joe.

He takes a slug out of one of the pints and puts them down. He begins to
press through the crowd. TARA takes his hand. JOE is a little uneasy with
this. But he presses on.

76.   INT. FOYER NIGHT

JOE and TARA come to the cloakroom, holding hands. They have to wait for a moment. TARA has her arm around his arm, standing close to him. At the main entrance, the BOUNCERS are closing the door.

                    BOUNCER 2
          No! We're full! That's it! Go on!

                     VOICES
          'You fucking bastard!' Etc.

A bottle smashes against the half open door. Glass showers in. The BOUNCERS shut the door. It's like a siege.

                  BOUNCERS 1 & 2
              (To people in the foyer)
          Come on, move in please. Move in.
          Thank you.

                      JOE
          What's your bag like?

                     TARA
          It's a small black one.

                      JOE
                 (To ATTENDANT)
          Sorry. Has someone handed in a small
          black handbag?

                     TARA
          It's not a fucking handbag.

                      JOE
          What?

                   BOUNCER 1
          Come on. Move in or get out.

                      JOE
          She's lost her bag.

                   BOUNCER 1
          No. You get it at the end.

                   ATTENDANT
          I'm not looking for a bag now, Tony, I'm
          going on my break.

                   BOUNCER 1
          I know, come on, move in.

                              JOE
                    She's lost her stuff, man.

                           BOUNCER 1
                    There's nothing I can do about it. She's
                    wrecked.

                           BOUNCER 2
                    How much has she had to drink? How
                    much have you had to drink, love?

                              TARA
                    Oh, fuck off.

BOUNCER 1 grabs both of them.

                           BOUNCER 1
                    That's it. Out.

                              JOE
                    What?

                           BOUNCER 1
                    Darren, get the door.

BOUNCER 2 opens the door.

                           BOUNCER 1
                    Yous clean up your fucking act.

77.   EXT. SHADOWS NIGHT

JOE and TARA are lashed out the door. It slams behind them. JOE stands
there, bewildered. He bangs on the door.

                              JOE
                    I have my jacket in there!

A group of OLDER TEENAGERS hang around outside. One of them,
JUNIOR, approaches JOE.

                             JUNIOR
                    Here, you. What's your game?

                              JOE
                    What?

                             JUNIOR
                    Are you starting?

                              JOE
                    No.

                    JUNIOR
Do you want your go, do you?

                    OTHERS
Go on, Junior.

                    JOE
I'm just trying to get my coat.

                    JUNIOR
Don't get smart, I'll smack you round,
right? (Pause) What's your name?

                    JOE
                (Pause)
Joe.

                    JUNIOR
Joe what? Blow job?

                    TARA
Leave him alone.

                    OTHERS
'Woah. Watch it Junior.' Etc

                    JUNIOR
Sorry. Are you talking to me, Tits?
'Cause I'll slap the fucking head off
you and all.

                    TARA
Yeah. Come on then.

She approaches JUNIOR.

                    OTHERS
'Wooo . . . Look out.' Etc.

                    JUNIOR
            (Strangely reasonable)
Because I have no fucking problem
with that, love.

TARA suddenly punches him right on the nose. He is hurt and stunned
for a moment, but then attacks TARA viciously. JOE goes to pull him
away, and is immediately set upon by the others, kicks and digs flying
into him from all sides. He pushes his way through this and grabs
TARA. [They run across the car park. Some of the gang pursue them,   ㉔
throwing really hard digs.

VOICE
Don't fucking come back, you fucking
bastards.]

78. EXT. BEACH NIGHT

JOE takes TARA to some rocks. They sit down.

                    JOE
        Are you okay?

                    TARA
        Yeah. I'm really sore. I'm really sorry.

                    JOE
        Show me your mouth.

He lifts her face to the light.

                    TARA
        Are you going to kiss it better?   ㉕

                    JOE
        [My fucking heart.] You got a fair right
        couple of smacks off your man.

                    TARA
        I see you every morning.

                    JOE
        I see you.

                    TARA
        I want to go asleep.

She leans into him. He sits with his arm around her.

                    DAMIEN
        Yo! Joe!

JOE is startled.

                    DAMIEN
        It's me. I have your bike.

                    JOE
        Jesus. I thought you were someone
        else.

                    [DAMIEN
        What happened?

69

JOE
We got fucked out. And then we got
the shit kicked out of us.

DAMIEN
That was you got in the fight?

JOE
Nah, just . . . fucking . . . we should get
her home.

DAMIEN
I know her.

JOE
Yeah?

DAMIEN
Yeah, I know where she lives. Come on.

JOE
I have to wait and get my coat. And her
bag and all.

DAMIEN
Get it tomorrow, man. There's still
loads of heads all up there.

JOE
Okay. Thanks for the bike. You go on
back in, if you want.

DAMIEN
Nah, I'm not bothered. There's fuck-all
action in there tonight.

JOE
What's her name?

DAMIEN
I think it's Tara.

JOE
Tara? Tara?] We'll take you home.

DAMIEN
Is she alright?

JOE
I think she's just a bit pissed more
than anything.

DAMIEN
Fucking typical.

79.   EXT. SECLUDED ROAD NIGHT

JOE and DAMIEN wheel their bikes up a dark winding lane with high trees. TARA leans into JOE, half asleep and half awake.

> DAMIEN
> Here, d'you want me to carry her for a while?

> JOE
> She's alright.

> DAMIEN
> Jays, you'll be wrecked. Come on.

DAMIEN stops. JOE tilts TARA towards him. TARA is reluctant.

> DAMIEN
> Come on. Give Joe a rest. That's it. I've got you.

They continue up the hill.

> JOE
> Does she live around here?

> DAMIEN
> Nah. This is a short cut. Listen, you go on. I can get her back.

> JOE
> Ah. I'll hang on with you.

80.   EXT. RUINED CHURCH NIGHT

They pass an old churchyard. DAMIEN holds TARA around the waist. He stops.

> DAMIEN
> Here. I got to have a piss. Hold my bike?

> JOE
> Is she okay?

> DAMIEN
> Yeah, she's alright. I'll just go in here.

DAMIEN leads TARA into the graveyard.

> JOE
> She can wait here with me.

DAMIEN keeps going. Pause.

                                    JOE
                She should wait out here, man. (Pause)
                Are yous alright, yeah?

Long pause. JOE gets restless. He wheels the bikes into the graveyard.

81.   EXT. GRAVEYARD NIGHT   ㉖

JOE stands with the bikes in the graveyard. The wind rustles the leaves.

                                  [JOE
                Damien?

He hears a soft sound. A whimper, possibly.

                                    JOE
                Damien?]

JOE moves towards the sound. Coming around the headstones, he sees
something moving on a grave. He goes nearer. What he sees is DAMIEN's
bare arse moving up and down. TARA's legs are on either side of him. Her
head hangs over the low rail around the grave. She lies there quite limply.
JOE looks at this for a moment. He drops DAMIEN's bike and cycles away.

82.   EXT. ROAD NIGHT

JOE pedals madly down the road.

83.   INT. BATHROOM NIGHT   ㉗

JOE gets sick in the toilet.

[84.   INT. BEDROOM NIGHT   ㉘

JOE comes in. FRANK is asleep. JOE picks up the picture of his mother,
and looks at her. He holds the picture and lies down fully clothed.]

                TITLE BOARD: 'Thursday'

85.   EXT. COAST DAY

JOE cycles to school. TARA isn't at the bus stop.

86.   INT. CLASSROOM DAY

JOE is in hell. He sits restlessly, fidgeting. The place beside him is empty.
No DAMIEN.

INT. CHIPPER DAY

It is very quiet. FRANK is wiping the tables. He looks over at GEORGE. GEORGE is reading the paper.]

88.   INT. BEDROOM DAY

FRANK takes a suitcase from under the bed. He opens it. He takes a parka jacket out, and the hat from a pocket. The 'gun' and gloves are wrapped in a pillowcase. He puts the gun down his pants. He puts on the jacket and the gloves He puts the hat on top of his head.

[89.   INT. CHIPPER DAY

FRANK peeps at GEORGE. GEORGE is still reading the paper. FRANK goes out the back.]

90.   EXT. YARD DAY

FRANK comes out the back and crosses the yard.

91.   EXT. STREET DAY

FRANK comes down the street to the seafront. The road is deserted.

92.   EXT. SEAFRONT DAY

FRANK walks down the bookies. He pauses. He watches a car turn the corner. He takes a deep breath. He pulls the hat down over his face, takes the 'gun', and goes inside.

93.   INT. BOOKIES DAY   ㉚

Over the speaker a race starts. CHARLIE sits on a stool watching the teletext. SIMON drinks from a cup of tea and writes in a ledger. TWO OLD MEN fill in dockets. ORLA, the clerk, holds a sheet of paper and writes odds on a wallchart with a marker. FRANK stands there. No-one notices him.

                              FRANK
                 Alright. Nodiddy fuckdinove.

Pause. The others stand looking at him.

                              SIMON
            What?

                              FRANK
                 Nobody fucking move.

SIMON

What are you doing?

FRANK

(Shouts)

Nobody fucking move! This is a
robbery! Put your fucking hands up!

ORLA hesitantly raises her hands. The OLD MEN just stare. FRANK
suddenly kicks CHARLIE's stool. CHARLIE falls heavily to the floor.

FRANK

The rest a yous down as well, come on.

SIMON is looking for somewhere to put his cup. FRANK slaps his hand.

FRANK

Just . . . put the fucking thing down!

FRANK pins SIMON to the wall with the barrel of the 'gun'. The OLD MEN
struggle to get on to the ground.

FRANK

Just get down.

ORLA lies on the floor.

FRANK

Put your hands behind your heads.
Faces on the on the floor. (To SIMON)
Okay. I want every penny in the place.

He pushes SIMON away towards the counter.

SIMON

It's not much, son. It won't be worth
your while.

FRANK sticks the 'gun' under SIMON's chin.

FRANK

You better make it worth my while, you
fat bastard. Get in there.

FRANK pushes SIMON in behind the counter. Then he jumps up on it
where he can see everything. SIMON tries to open the till. He can't.

SIMON

Orla . . .

ORLA

Bang it on the side.

                         SIMON
                       (Hitting it)
       Where?

                          ORLA
              With your right. No. Yeah.

                         SIMON
               Make up your mind.

SIMON gets the till open. He takes out whatever there is. It doesn't look
like much. He hands it to FRANK. FRANK puts it in his pocket.

                         SIMON
              Now, you've got what you want. Come
              on, get out.

                         FRANK
              No. I want the safe.

                         SIMON
              What safe?

FRANK points the 'gun' at CHARLIE.

                         FRANK
              If you don't open the safe now, I'll blow
              his legs off.

                       OLD MAN
       Yes!

                         FRANK
       What?

                       OLD MAN
              Sorry. I'm after winning.

The results are announced. FRANK turns his attention back to SIMON.

                         FRANK
              I mean it. I'll cripple him.

                         SIMON
              Don't do anything stupid.

                         FRANK
              That's up to you.

SIMON considers. Then he moves towards the office.

                         FRANK
              Leave the door open.

FRANK watches SIMON kneel at the safe.

                        [FRANK
                    (To OLD MAN)
          How much did you win?

                        OLD MAN
          Two sixty.

                        FRANK
          Big win.

                        OLD MAN
          It's not bad.

FRANK crumples up one of the notes SIMON gave him and throws it to the
OLD MAN. It bounces off his head.

                        FRANK
          Sorry.

                        OLD MAN
          Thanks.]

SIMON comes out with two envelopes.

                        FRANK
          Okay. Come round.

SIMON comes out into the shop. FRANK takes the envelopes and shoves
them in his pocket.

                        SIMON
          Are you happy now, big man?

                        FRANK
                    (Pause)
          Take your clothes off.

                        SIMON
          Excuse me?

FRANK points the 'gun' at SIMON's crotch.

                        FRANK
          It's that or no bollocks.

                        SIMON
          Take it easy.

                        FRANK
          It is easy.

                        SIMON
          You're mad.

                          76

FRANK
(A word of advice)
You should do it then.

SIMON opens his shirt.

FRANK
I don't have all day.

SIMON takes his shirt off and stands there in his vest.

FRANK
All off.

SIMON
What, you want my cacks off and
everything? What's wrong with you?

FRANK
Just do it.

SIMON
No.

SIMON and FRANK look at each other.

FRANK
Do it.

SIMON
No I'm not. (Pause) I'm not doing it.

FRANK pushes SIMON.

FRANK
Take your fucking clothes off.

SIMON
No, I'm not gonna do it.

FRANK pushes him again.

SIMON
I'm not gonna do it. You're wasting
your time. So just fucking get out.
Right? Just get out. (Pause) I'll take
my shoes and socks off.

SIMON takes off one shoe and sock. FRANK grabs SIMON and takes him
to the door. He opens the door and has a look.

EXT. STREET DAY   ㉛

FRANK looks out of the bookies. The street is empty. He reappears with
SIMON. He slams the door behind them.

                                    FRANK
                    See you later.

FRANK runs around the corner. SIMON is banging on the door of the
bookies.

                                    SIMON
                    Let me in! He's gone! Come on, he's
                    gone!

95.   EXT. YARD 2 DAY

FRANK runs across the yard at the back of the bookies. He runs over to the
wall. He climbs up on a bin and grabs the top of the wall.

                                    CHARLIE
                    Hey!

FRANK sees CHARLIE running towards him. CHARLIE has a machete.
FRANK points the 'gun' at him.

                                    FRANK
                    Don't fucking move . . .

CHARLIE hesitates.

                                    FRANK
                    Turnaround. Turnaround!

CHARLIE wants to attack FRANK. But the tiniest doubt holds him back.
He hates it. He turns around. FRANK throws the 'gun' over the wall. He
catches his heel at the top and pulls himself up. CHARLIE can't bear it. He
turns around and runs at the wall. FRANK panics and falls over the wall.

96.   EXT. LANE DAY

FRANK lands pretty badly. He gets himself up. He is hurt.

97.   EXT. YARD 2 DAY

CHARLIE gets up on the bin. He falls in the bin. The bin falls over.

98.   EXT. LANE DAY

FRANK puts the 'gun' in his pants and limps away.

99.   EXT. YARD 2 DAY

CHARLIE rights the bin. He gets up and grabs the top of the wall.

100.   EXT. LANE DAY

FRANK walks down the lane. He pulls the hat off.

101.   EXT. MAIN STREET DAY

FRANK comes out into the street. There aren't many people. FRANK tries to walk normally and breathe slowly. He looks back at the lane. He looks around for somewhere to hide. He tries a pub door. It is shut. He keeps walking. RAY's car pulls over. RAY leans over and opens the passenger door.

                    RAY
         Yo! Frank!

                    FRANK
         Ray!

FRANK gets in.

102.   INT. CAR DAY

                    RAY
         Are you okay?

                    FRANK
         Just go!

                    RAY
         What?

                    FRANK
         GO! Just go! Just go!

FRANK makes himself small.

                    RAY
         Okay, just cool it.

RAY pulls away.

103.   EXT. MAIN STREET DAY

JOE comes around the corner on his bike. As he passes the lane, CHARLIE comes running out and knocks him over. They go flying in a heap.

                    JOE
         What are you fucking doing?

CHARLIE looks up and down the street. All is quiet.

[104. EXT. YARD DAY.   ㉜

JOE wheels into the yard, the chain is off, he leaves it.]

105. INT. LANDING DAY

JOE tries his bedroom door. It is locked.

                         JOE
              Frank?

106. INT. BEDROOM DAY   ㉝

FRANK and RAY stand looking at a pile of money on the bed. Some of it
has fallen on to the floor They are breathless. They look at each other.
RAY shrugs helplessly.

107. INT. LANDING DAY

JOE knocks on the door again.

                         JOE
              Frank?

                        FRANK
                     (Behind door)
              Joe?

                         JOE
              Yeah.

FRANK opens the door and pulls JOE in.

108. INT. BEDROOM DAY

RAY stands looking out the window. FRANK puts JOE on the floor and sits
on him. JOE is on some money.

                         JOE
              What's . . .

                        FRANK
              Look at me.

                         JOE
              What?

                        FRANK
              Look at me now.

JOE

What's wrong?

FRANK

I'm after stealing some money.

JOE

What?

FRANK

I'm after stealing some money from
Simple Simon.

JOE

(Knows FRANK's tone is serious)
Frank, don't fucking mess, man, what
is it?

FRANK

I'm not messing. You know Dad owed
Simple Simon money.

JOE

What money?

FRANK

He owes him some money.

JOE

How much? How much is it?

(34)

FRANK

[We think I'm after getting about thirty
grand.] I'm being straight with you,
Joe. I'm being fucking straight with you
here, right?

JOE

This is a joke. Ray. This is your money.

RAY

I wish it was. I'm after doing the
getaway.

JOE

Yous both did it?

FRANK

No. He didn't know.

RAY

No it was . . .

81

[FRANK.
I was blessed. Charlie nearly caught me.

JOE
Just now?

FRANK
Ten minutes ago.

JOE
He's after knocking me off my bike.

FRANK
(Terror)
What?

JOE
No. He came out of the lane and ran
into me.

FRANK
Just now?

JOE
Yeah.

FRANK
Yous both fucking saved me. Do you
know that?]

JOE
I've got to get out of here.

JOE heaves FRANK off him and makes for the door. FRANK pushes it
closed. It hits JOE on the head. They all feel it. JOE holds his head.

JOE
Hssss.

FRANK
I'm sorry. I'm sorry. Joe. I'm sorry. Sit
down.

RAY
Sore . . .

JOE
My fucking head.

FRANK
Shh . . . You'll be alright in a minute.

JOE
What are we supposed to do?

RAY
(Gathering money)
See, someone's finally asking a
sensible question. And I should know.
I have that sort of philosophical
training.

[109.   EXT. STREET DAY   ㉟

RAY drives up the street, past the bookies. Three heads, FRANK, RAY and
JOE, crane for a look. There are squad cars and GUARDS. A group of
WOMEN stand talking about it. Another more official-looking woman
takes notes. She is the detective, Sgt DUGGAN. She senses something.
She looks up and makes eye contact with FRANK.

110.   EXT. COAST DAY

RAY, FRANK and JOE stand near the car, leaning on a railing, looking out
at the sea.

RAY
They wouldn't have recognised you . . .

FRANK
No.

JOE
Did you put on a funny voice?

FRANK.
Don't be fucking stupid.

JOE
What are you gonna do?

RAY.
Absolutely nothing is what you're
gonna do. You take off they'll know it
was you. Go back to work.

FRANK
Go back to work?

RAY
Go back to work. 'Everything's fine.'
Listen to what the local theories are.
And cultivate them.

FRANK
Take my chances here . . .

                         RAY
              Yeah. Great. I mean, I really don't need
              this crap. Thanks Frank. Brilliant

    RAY goes back to the car. FRANK and JOE look at each other.]

111.   INT. CHIPPER DAY

    FRANK and JOE sit rather subdued. They're almost afraid to move in case
    they attract attention. GEORGE brings over their dinner.

                         GEORGE
              Is everything alright?

                         FRANK
              Yeah . . .

                         GEORGE
              Yous both . . . You look like you've seen
              a ghost.

                          JOE
              Nah, I just saw a dog being knocked
              down.

                         GEORGE
              A dog? You'd think it was a child, the
              way you're sitting there.

                         FRANK
              Ah he's . . .

    GEORGE tousles JOE's hair.

                         GEORGE
              Tuh. What's wrong with your leg?

                         FRANK
              Ah. I was trying to help the dog. He bit
              me.

                         GEORGE
              Fucking . . . Get it seen to, boy.

                         FRANK
              Yeah . . . I'll go down after tea.

    FRANK and JOE exchange a look.

We see their bedside clock. It is 5.45 am. FRANK and JOE are in bed.

                         JOE
        Frank?

                        FRANK
        Yeah?

                         JOE
        I haven't slept all night.

                        FRANK
        I know.

                         JOE
        Did you have a knife or something?

                        FRANK
        I had a . . . Come on man. Just . . . It's
        better if we don't

                         JOE
        Okay. What are you going to do with
        the money?

                        FRANK
        I'm thinking about it.

                         JOE
        Yeah?

                        FRANK
        But . . . I'm not talking about it.

                         JOE
        Yeah. (Pause) Good.

JOE idly looks at the photos on their locker. Their mother, another young
woman.

                         JOE
        Do you see her any more?

                        FRANK
        Nah . . . She's in America.

                         JOE
        I remember you driving her around
        when you had the ice-cream van.

FRANK
(Pause)
I felt like a fucking monkey in that van.

JOE
Got you around. And the ice-cream
and all.

FRANK
(Wearily)
Yeah. The ice-cream. Brilliant.

JOE
Why did you feel like a monkey?

FRANK
Because you'd be parked down the
causeway or somewhere, down the
beach, having a bit of nookie. Everyone
knew where you were. Big ice-cream
van. Everyone knew what you were up
to.

JOE
Why do you keep her picture?

FRANK
I don't know. It's just something I do.
I'll have to get rid of it.

JOE
I like it.

FRANK
Yeah?

JOE
Yeah, she was nice.

FRANK
Yeah.]

TITLE BOARD: 'Friday'

113. EXT. COAST DAY

JOE cycles to school. He looks at the bus stop. No TARA.

114. INT. CHIPPER (SIT DOWN PART) DAY ㊲

FRANK sits reading the paper. He reads page three. The plainclothes policewoman, SGT DUGGAN comes in.

DUGGAN
Hello.

FRANK
How're you? What can I get you?

DUGGAN
No, no. Sit down. I'm not hungry. I'm
just noseying around.

FRANK
Okay.

DUGGAN
How's your dad?

FRANK
He's fine thanks, yeah.

DUGGAN
Is he around?

FRANK
He's having a bit of a nap.

DUGGAN
Well. It's quiet, isn't it?

FRANK
It is, this time of the year, yeah.

DUGGAN
Business is slow.

FRANK
Yeah, it's, it's okay . . .

DUGGAN
You keep ticking over . . .

FRANK
We manage. You have to, you know?

DUGGAN
Yeah, you don't want to run into debt.

FRANK
Yeah. I leave all that to my father.

DUGGAN
Were you working yesterday?

FRANK
Ah you know. I'm here most days.

                    DUGGAN
                 (Direct but fair)
          Do you know anything about the
          robbery?

                     FRANK
          About the bookies?

                    DUGGAN
          Mmm.

                     FRANK
          Do I know what about it?

                    DUGGAN
          I just thought you might have heard
          about it.

                     FRANK
          Just the same as anyone. Someone
          held it up.

                    DUGGAN
          It was someone fairly young. Fairly
          athletic.

She looks at his strapped-up leg. He cannot help shifting it under the table
a little.

                     FRANK
          Yeah?

                    DUGGAN
          There's not that young a population
          around here. Is there?

                     FRANK
          I don't know. All up the Grange there.
          The new estates.

                    DUGGAN
          I mean around here. All the drunk old
          men. You think one of them could've
          done it?

                     FRANK
          No, it's a pretty old population around
          here.

She shows him a photograph of JOHN TRAYNOR.

                    DUGGAN
          You know this young buck, don't you?

FRANK
Yeah. John Traynor.

DUGGAN
Have you seen him since he left prison?

FRANK
I had a pint with him.

DUGGAN
He's broken his parole. Did you know
that?

FRANK
No.

DUGGAN
Did he say anything to you about
leaving?

FRANK.
Em. I think he might have said
something about going to Chicago,
or something like that.

DUGGAN
Chicago . . .

FRANK
I don't remember.

DUGGAN
Did he have any money?

FRANK
I don't know.

DUGGAN
Did he say anything about the
bookies?

FRANK
No.

DUGGAN
You didn't talk about it?

FRANK
No.

DUGGAN
I want you to have a think about it.
And give me a call if you remember
anything. Will you do that?

She gives FRANK a card.

> FRANK
> Sure. Do you think he had anything to
> do with it?

> DUGGAN
> I'm just noseying around, Frank.

> FRANK
> Okay.

> DUGGAN
> Give me a ring anyway, if you want
> I'll leave you to your paper.

She gets up. FRANK looks down at page three. He puts his cup over the model's breasts.

> FRANK
> (Chuckles, embarrassed)
> It's not mine. Somebody left it.

> DUGGAN
> Finders keepers.

She leaves. FRANK lights a cigarette.

[115.   EXT. DAMIEN'S HOUSE DAY

JOE is ringing and banging on the door. He shouts hello and peers through a window. No-one home. He leaves.]

116.   INT. RAY'S OFFICE DAY

RAY is reading books on Konigsberg. The phone rings. It's FRANK.

> FRANK
> Ray, man.

> RAY
> Frank. How's it going?

> FRANK
> Fucking nerve-racking man.

> RAY
> How's Joe?

> FRANK
> He's okay. He's good.

RAY

Yeah?

FRANK

Yeah, but I sort of don't know what I'm
doing.

RAY

You're not doing anything.

FRANK

I got to do something, man.

RAY

Like what?

FRANK.

I can't even . . .

GEORGE passes. FRANK lowers his voice.

FRANK

I want to get away.

RAY stiffens.

FRANK

I've got to get out of here. Couple of
days, even.

RAY

Okay. We'll go away for the weekend.
We'll bring Joe. Nice hotel. Pool. Yeah . . .

FRANK

Yeah. Good.

RAY

I'll pick you up tomorrow. Around
lunchtime, yeah?

FRANK

Yeah. Good. Okay

RAY

And Frank. This is on you.

FRANK

Of course it's on me.

RAY

Fucking right 'Of course it is . . . ', you
fucking moron

ACADEMICS and STUDENTS are gathered in a room drinking wine and eating sandwiches. RAY milling wine. He slugs a glass back in one go and picks up another. He sees DEBORAH on the other side of the room. She stands with a group, she tries to catch his eve. TONY REGAN comes over to RAY.

> TONY
> Ray. Good man. Come here to me.
> Listen, I'm sorry things didn't go your
> way at the meeting.

> RAY
> Tony, I'm sorry I lost my temper.

> TONY
> Ah, a bit of passion. What the hell? But
> the thing is when we met him at the
> airport, he's a nice enough fella, I said
> it to him about a few little questions, lo
> and behold, he just goes, 'Fine.'

> RAY
> After all that?

> TONY
> Ah, it's not a session, now. He'll take a
> few quick questions. And I have you . . .
> that you'll ask one.

> RAY
> No it's brilliant. That's great, Tony.
> Thanks. This is what it's about, you
> know?

> TONY
> No I'm looking forward to it. Oh. There
> he is.

They look over at a small bespectacled man, KONIGSBERG, who is talking with a group of academics.

> TONY
> I better go over and do my duty. Do
> you want to meet him?

> RAY
> No. I'll save myself for the big picture.

TONY
(Laughs)
Okay, fair enough. Eleven in the
morning, alright? Don't drink too much.

RAY
Yeah.

TONY leaves. RAY sees TRISH MEEHAN coming over to him. He turns
away and lowers a glass of wine, picks up another one.

TRISH
That's it. Don't mind me. A little drink
in moderation never hurt anyone.

RAY
Why the hell do you always look at me
like I just gingerly slipped a wasp up
your crack?

TRISH
Because I know what you're like,
maybe.

RAY
Look, I know, it's a terrible thing.
You've gone through your whole life,
no one'll come near you with a ten-foot
pole. But it's nobody's fault. It's not the
fault of mankind, Trish. Let it go.

TRISH
I'm going to be a little bit more
specific. I had a student visit me today.
Very concerned about the relationship
between you and a third year, Deborah
McCeever, being inappropriate.

RAY sees DEBORAH.

TRISH
Tell me about you and Deborah
McCeever. Oh, that got your attention.
What are you playing at?

RAY
You have no idea what you 're talking
about.

TRISH
Oh really? Then why has one of her
classmates reported you?

> RAY
>
> (Helpless)
>
> What do you want me to do? What
> would make you happy in this
> situation, Trish?

> TRISH
>
> Sort it out, Ray. Don't make me tell Tony.

RAY regards TRISH, then he lowers his glass of wine.

> RAY
>
> Trish. I'm going to do it for you. Do you
> know why?

> TRISH
>
> Why?

> RAY
>
> Because you may not have a nice
> appearance or demeanour, or . . .
> anything, you have a fantastic little
> arse thing going on there. And it just
> about saves you.

> TRISH
>
> There's nothing you can say to offend
> me, Ray. Because I think your opinion
> is worthless.

> RAY
>
> Trish. It's only mischief.

[He winks at her and walks away. he approaches DEBORAH, greeting one
or two people is he goes.]

> RAY
>
> [Hi, how's it going?] (To DEBORAH)
> Listen, I think we should go
> somewhere, and have a chat, yeah?

She nods and they leave. TONY REGAN watches them leave. He then
turns back to the people he's with. They all listen to KONIGSBERG.

118.   INT. STUDENT BAR NIGHT   ㊴

RAY brings drinks to where DEBORAH sits.

> RAY
>
> Deborah, I'm in trouble with my boss.
> And so are you. It's an extremely bad
> situation.

DEBORAH

What, I'm in trouble?

RAY

The only way I'm going to be allowed
to keep my job is if you get booted out
of college.

DEBORAH

What?!

RAY

Or – we stop seeing other.

DEBORAH

Jesus Christ!

RAY

So what do you want to do?

DEBORAH

Ray, I can't believe they'd boot me out.

RAY

Yes, absolutely they'd boot you out.

DEBORAH

They would in their arse!

RAY

Believe what you like. you wouldn't be
the first. We have to stop seeing each
other. Forthwith. As of.

DEBORAH

Okay . . . Okay. Jesus Christ.

RAY

I know. Deborah, I think you're lovely.
(Pause). You don't have to return the
compliment.

DEBORAH

Sorry. I'm just fucking reeling here. I'm
in shock.

RAY

I know. So that's that. Sin é. Sin Sin.

DEBORAH

Okay. Jesus.

RAY places his hand on her shoulder. She pushes it away again. He does
it again. She pushes it away again.

                              RAY
          Can I have a hug?

                            DEBORAH
          Ray, we can't.

                              RAY
          Can I come back to your house?

                            DEBORAH
          I really don't think that's a very good
          idea.

119.   EXT. DEBORAH'S HOUSE NIGHT

RAY'S car pulls up. RAY and DEBORAH get out and rush towards the
house.

120.   SCENE DELETED

121.   INT. DEBORAH'S HOUSE NIGHT

They go up the stairs, pausing to lie on top of each other, then continuing
their journey.

122.   INT. BEDROOM NIGHT

RAY lies across the bed while DEBORAH undresses. His clothes are half
off. She is wearing a pair of knee-length boots.

                              RAY
               (Almost with dismay at himself)
          Listen, I'm really kind of interested in
          you keeping the boots on.

She pauses. A mischievous grin.

                            DEBORAH
          Okay.

They lie on the bed, kissing. [The door opens and VYVIAN steps in,   ④⓪
watching them. They don't notice him.

                            VYVIAN
          Get off her!

                            DEBORAH
          Vyvian!

VYVIAN approaches.

96

                              VYVIAN
                         Stay away from her!

RAY swings a punch, knocking VYVIAN to the floor. VYVIAN pulls a lamp
down with him. RAY tries to go. VYVIAN grabs RAY's feet. RAY falls and
pushes VYVIAN under the bed with his feet. VYVIAN is stuck. RAY gets up
and leaves.

123.   INT. LANDING NIGHT

RAY comes to the stairs, trying to pull trousers up. He falls to the bottom
of the stairs.

124.   SCENE DELETED

125.   EXT. DEBORAH'S HOUSE NIGHT

RAY fumbles with his keys trying to unlock his car. He drops the keys.
VYVIAN comes down the driveway with a golf club.

                              RAY
                         Fucking hell.

RAY picks up his keys and gets the door open. He gets in.

                              VYVIAN
                    Who do you fucking think you are?

VYVIAN whacks the windscreen.

126.   INT. CAR NIGHT

RAY starts the engine. The windscreen cracks. VYVIAN pauses. He seems
surprised. RAY has had enough.

                              RAY
                         Fucking hell.

RAY turns off the engine. VYVIAN stands there. RAY opens the door
violently, knocking VYVIAN to the ground. RAY gets out.

                              RAY
                       (Picks up golf club)
                    Look what you're after doing!

                              VYVIAN
                          (Placatory)
                      Okay. Okay. Okay.

VYVIAN gets up, moving away. RAY follows him.

                                97

                         RAY
              What's your fucking problem?

EXT. GARDEN NIGHT

     VYVIAN goes into a garden next door. RAY follows him.

                         RAY
              What's wrong with you?

     VYVIAN rings the doorbell.

                        VYVIAN
              I'm . . . I'm sorry . . . I didn't . . . I didn't

                         RAY
              This is unbelievable.

                        VYVIAN
              I know, I know.

                         RAY
              Did you see my fucking car?

                        VYVIAN
              Look I know. I'm . . . I'm . . . I love her.

     RAY just looks at him.

     The door opens. A woman in a dressing gown stands there.

                        WOMAN
              What's going on? What are you doing?

     RAY looks at the woman.

                        VYVIAN
              I'm so

     RAY turns and walks away.

                        WOMAN
                       (To VYVIAN)
              Are you alright?

     DEBORAH comes to the gate.

                       DEBORAH
              Ray . . .

                         RAY
              You should . . . Do some studying

     RAY leaves. DEBORAH goes towards VYVIAN.

127.   DELETE

128.   DELETE

129.   DELETE

130.   DELETE

133.   INT. RAY'S FLAT NIGHT

RAY sits on hi bed. He has a bottle of whiskey and a glass. He lowers
two large shots of whiskey. He looks at the glass. He looks at the bottle.
He drops the glass and drinks from the bottle.]

TITLE BOARD: 'Saturday'

134.   INT. CHIPPER LIVING QUARTERS DAY

GEORGE comes down the landing. There is a ladder up to the attic.

GEORGE
(Shouts up)
What are yous doing?

FRANK
Just getting a suitcase!

GEORGE
What time are yous going?

FRANK
Ray's picking us up at lunchtime.

135.   INT. ATTIC DAY

JOE and FRANK are putting plastic bags full of money behind a loose
brick in the wall. FRANK opens the bag and takes some money out.

JOE
How much are you taking?

FRANK
I'm only guessing, and we want to do
this properly. (Short pause) I'm taking
five grand.

[136.   INT. CHIPPER (TAKE-AWAY PART) DAY   ㊶

FRANK is working. Two town drinkers are in the queue, LARRY & MACK.

> LARRY
> Oh Jaysus . . . Is this gonna be long,
> Frank? I'm after being in Reynold's all
> morning. I'm dying for a Jimmy Riddle.

> FRANK
> It's only going to be a minute.

> LARRY
> Jaysus, just while I'm waiting, where's
> the . . .

He makes two short little whistles, meaning, 'toilet.'

> FRANK
> Where's the what . . . ? The 'referee?'

> LARRY
> Ah Frank, come on. I'm fucking dying.

FRANK sees SIMPLE SIMON and CHARLIE come into the sit-down part of the chipper.

> FRANK
> (Distracted)
> Go round, it's at the back.

> LARRY
> Yo ho. You're a life saver.

LARRY does a little dance.

> FRANK
> Yeah . . .]

137.   INT. CHIPPER (SIT-DOWN PART) DAY

FRANK brings food over to SIMPLE SIMON.

> FRANK
> How are yous?

> SIMON.
> Ah . . .

> FRANK
> It's shocking, what happened.

> SIMON
> It's a dreadful fucking world, Frank.
> You put years into a community. You
> turn around, they fuck you in the arse.

FRANK
Do you think they'll ever catch who
did it?

SIMON
Are you codding me? The guards in
this town couldn't catch the clap off a
ten-spot whore.

CHARLIE
The fucking killer is, I nearly had the
bastard, Frank. I was about as close to
him as I am to you now.

FRANK
Yeah?

SIMON
Vanished into thin air, Frank. Luckiest
bastard I ever saw.

We can see that FRANK knows just how true this is. What he says next
could be about SIMON and CHARLIE or robbers.

FRANK
Bastards . . .

138.   INT. RAY'S BEDROOM MORNING

The alarm clock is ringing for ages. RAY wakes up. The whiskey bottle is
empty beside him. He looks at it. He can hardly move.

RAY
Oh Jesus Christ.

139.   INT. BATHROOM MORNING

RAY sits on the toilet, half awake. Horrible, low, ominous sounds emanate
from his arse. He falls asleep. He falls off the toilet. He wakes just as he
hits the floor. He lets out a little helpless cry.

[140.   INT. CAR MORNING   ㊷

RAY drives to college.]

141.   EXT. GARAGE MORNING

RAY leans on his car. Hands shaking, he opens a box of aspirin and pops
some in his mouth. He then opens a large carton of orange juice. He puts
it to his mouth and slugs away, almost uncontrollably.

142.   INT. LECTURE HALL DAY

The lecture hall is full of students. People even sit on the steps.
KONIGSBERG's lecture is already in progress. RAY makes his way to
a bench.

> KONIGSBERG
> When I say that language is dying, the
> most common criticism is that I
> couldn't communicate such a fact if it
> were. Further, all I am in fact doing by
> saying language is an organic thing
> which can die is using a pretty poor
> metaphor.

RAY excuses himself past people and finds an empty seat in the middle of
a row. TONY REGAN looks up at RAY. RAY gives him a little smile. While
the lecture continues:

> But what my critics must ask
> themselves, is this: Isn't it easy to see
> everything we disagree with as a poor
> metaphor? Indeed when do we stop
> using metaphor in place of valid
> reason?

RAY looks dreadful. He is finding it hard simply staying awake. He sees
DEBORAH. She looks away.

> On both the left and right of politics for
> instance, we can only seek to expose
> bad policies in terms of their projected
> outcomes. 'The poor will be poorer in
> the land you wish to create,' we say.
> What land is this? It is a metaphorical
> land where we are powerless to stop
> our enemies. 'But thank God we are in
> the real world where we can stop
> them,' we say, 'Because we do not live
> in a metaphorical world.' But if we can
> only make our point through metaphor
> and imagination, by creatively telling
> each other what statistics and hard
> data actually mean, what facts mean,
> we are living in a world of metaphor.

RAY closes his eyes.

> And I do concede that when I claim
> that language is dying, I am being
> partly mischievous, but this has been

said before. Socrates was concerned by
the sophist's mastery of rhetoric for
precisely this reason. The more
communication becomes an effective
tool in getting us what we want, the
more selective we become with
information the less we can really
know. And that is all I mean. Thank
you very much.

By this time RAY has fallen asleep. The lecture-hall erupts in applause.
RAY is startled, he claps. TONY REGAN takes the podium.

> ### TONY
> Thank you, Professor Konigsberg.
> I think we all agree that his lectures
> have, for those familiar with his work,
> clarified many points, while serving as
> a lucid introduction for those less
> familiar. And it's been quite a
> privilege, thank you very much. Now,
> Professor Konigsberg has very kindly
> agreed to take one or two questions,
> and I know that Dr Raymond Sullivan
> would like to ask the first one.

RAY is looking particularly nauseous. He takes a few deep breaths and
gets to his feet. People look at him expectantly. He swallows hard.
Suddenly his face is a picture of bewilderment and surprise. He opens his
mouth and a long stream of orange puke shoots out. He gets all the people
in front of him for about ten feet, including TRISH MEEHAN. It's not very
nice. Panic and disgust is registered in the faces of his victims. Then it's
over. There is complete silence. RAY looks a lot better. He wipes his
mouth.

> ### RAY
> Yes, thank you, Professor Regan. I
> would like to ask Professor Konigsberg
> if, during his long, and eminent,
> career, he has ever seen anything
> expressed quite like that?

TONY REGAN doesn't know what to do. He just looks at KONIGSBERG.
KONIGSBERG just regards RAY, and then finally slowly shakes his head.

> ### RAY
> Thank you. This has certainly cleared
> up a lot for me. (To person beside him)
> Excuse me.

RAY makes his way out of the lecture-hall. Everyone sits in silence.

103

143.　EXT. CHIPPER DAY

FRANK and JOE put their overnight bags into RAY's boot. RAY leans on a barrier, looking at the sea. GEORGE comes out and takes FRANK aside offering him twenty pounds.

> FRANK
> Ah no here, I'm grand. No.

> GEORGE
> For a drink, would you buy a round and
> don't be messing.

GEORGE forces the money into FRANK's pocket. FRANK embraces him.

> GEORGE
> Steady on. You're only going for a
> night.

[144.　EXT. POSH HOTEL BY THE SEA IN THE COUNTRY DAY

RAY's car pulls in.

145.　INT. CAR DAY

They sit in the car and look at the hotel. RAY switches off the engine. They all look too wrecked to be excited.

> JOE
> What's it got?

> RAY
> Everything. Did you bring your golf
> clubs?

> JOE
> Can we hire golf clubs? Play golf?

> RAY
> All the way down here, it's like
> someone died in the fucking car. Let's
> go and forget our troubles. That's what
> I want to do, no more morose bastards.
> And I'm sorry, but golf just doesn't fit
> that fucking agenda.]

146.　INT. HOTEL LEISURE COMPLEX

FRANK sits alone in the Jacuzzi. A beautiful woman gets in and sits opposite him. He doesn't know where to look.

147.   INT. SAUNA DAY

RAY and JOE sit in the sauna, drinking.

                    JOE
          What do . . . girls want when they're . . .
          with a fella?

                    RAY
          Well. That's a hard question. It's like
          saying, what do people want. Nobody
          knows. But that's alright, isn't it?

                    JOE
          What if . . . Say a girl . . . was like . . .
          asleep or something like that, and you
          decided you were gonna, you know . . .
          do what you wanted, while she was
          asleep, or mad drunk or something.
          If she didn't know. She wouldn't want
          it would she?

                    RAY
          I think the thing about things like that
          is . . . just don't be a bollocks. Isn't it?
          But sometimes you just fucking . . .
          can't see past yourself, and you just . . .
          go on and be a bollocks anyway, and
          you know you are. And that might just
          make you annoyed and you keep
          going. But I'll tell you this much: I wish
          I'd respected women more in my life.
          Because nothing's worth ending up on
          your own for. Nothing. Make sure the
          girl's awake, and I kind of mean that
          about all things. Not just . . . physical
          em, desires. (Pause) But fuck . . . Long
          hair, big tits, gets me every time. Like
          I'm always fucking asleep or
          something.

They laugh a little. Not much.

148.   INT. NIGHTCLUB NIGHT

FRANK and JOE sit at a table watching the girls dance. RAY comes to the
table with a large bottle of champagne. They are all somewhat drunk.

                    RAY
          Den! Duh! Dah!

                         FRANK

Oh yeah . . .

                          RAY

Yeah. I think I want to celebrate. (To
JOE) Have you ever had champagne?

                          JOE

No.

                         FRANK

I haven't either.

                          RAY

What? Ah now here, come on. You
have to have some.

RAY works on the bottle. A WAITRESS brings a tray of glasses to their
table.

                          RAY

Thank you sweetheart, just plonk them
down there. You won't join us, no?
Okay. Thank you.

The cork flies off the bottle and hits someone on the back of the head,
bouncing high into the air. The people at the table look around,
bewildered. RAY is oblivious. He pours three glasses.

                          RAY

Now. Cheers.

                      FRANK / JOE

Cheers. / Good luck.

They have a drink.

                          RAY

Isn't that the most fucking gorgeous
taste?

                          JOE

It's very bitter.

                         FRANK

It's horrible.

                          RAY

Ah, come on! You're not trying! This is
champagne!

                         FRANK

I just don't like it.

RAY

I'm being nice. I'm not going to tell you
how much this cost me.

FRANK

I didn't ask you to buy it, mate.

RAY

I know you didn't. I'm going to drink it,
man. Don't worry about me.

FRANK

I'm not worried.

RAY

I know you're not.

FRANK

Well, I'm not.

RAY

I know you're not.

FRANK

Good. Because I'm not.

RAY

Fucking . . . A few bob, you're different.
I'm going to drink this. I don't care. I'm
going to drink it all.

FRANK

Good, do.

RAY

I am.

FRANK

I know. Good. Do.

RAY

I will.

FRANK

I know. Good.

RAY

Yeah.

JOE is watching a fantastic looking girl dancing.

RAY

What are you looking at?

                              JOE
            Nothing.

                              RAY
            You are so, man. That's what you need.

Pause. They all watch her. A slower set begins, people sit down.

                              RAY
            You don't think you'd stand a chance
            there, no?

                              JOE
                       ('As if . . . ')
            What do you think?

                              RAY
            I think she'd go for you big time, man.
            Hold on.

RAY gets up and walks across the dance floor.

                              JOE
            What are you doing? What's he doing?

                             FRANK
            Ah, he's just talking to the sexiest girl
            I ever seen in my life. Relax.

RAY is talking to the girl. She looks over. JOE hides.

                              JOE
            What's he doing?

                             FRANK
            It's too late. She saw you.

                              JOE
            What's he doing?

                            FRANK.
            They're coming over.

                              JOE
            Oh fuck.

RAY brings the girl to the table.

                              RAY
            Gentlemen. This is Michelle. Michelle,
            this is Frank, and this is Joe, I was
            telling you about.

MICHELLE
Hi. (To JOE:) Would you like to dance?

JOE
Yeah . . .

She takes his hand and brings him onto the dance floor.

FRANK
What did you say to her?

RAY
What?

FRANK
How did you do it?

RAY
Ah.

FRANK
Come on, man.

RAY
Trade secret.

FRANK
Did you pay her?

RAY
Give us some credit, would you?

FRANK
I'm . . . begging you to tell me what
you said to her, man.

RAY
I told her he has six months to live.

FRANK
Is she not afraid of catching what he
has, no?

RAY
She's not stupid. You can't catch
leukemia.

JOE and MICHELLE dance. They dance slowly. JOE hangs on for dear life.
She begins to kiss him gently. FRANK and RAY look on.

RAY rings CARMEL. She is very groggy, standing in the dark in her
nightclothes.

                    CARMEL
        Hello?

                    RAY
        Hi.

                    CARMEL
        Ray?

                    RAY
        How are you?

                    CARMEL
        What time is it?

                    RAY
        It's late.

                    CARMEL
        Is everything okay?

                    RAY
        I want you to come and stay with me.

                    CARMEL
        What, tonight?

                    RAY
        No. When I'm . . . I want you to stay
        with me for ages.

                    CARMEL
        Live with you?

                    RAY
        Don't put me through a whole . . . thing
        with this. It's very simple. I'm lovely,
        come and stay with me and I won't let
        you down. That's all.

                    CARMEL
        Okay.

                    RAY
        Thank you. Goodnight. Okay. Good.
        There's no more money.

He hangs up. He collects his spare money.

150.   INT. HOTEL CORRIDOR NIGHT

RAY, FRANK and JOE come down their corridor. It is late. They are very tired and drunk. They swig from the champagne bottle. They stop at their rooms.

                              RAY
                           (To JOE)
              Well. Beautiful. You handled that
              beautifully. The most beautiful girl in
              the whole place. Who was she with?
              She was with this guy, Frank.

                             FRANK
              I know.

                              RAY
              She wasn't with me. She wasn't with
              you. She was with Bazooka Joe. (Long
              drunken pause) Goodnight. I had a
              good time. I'm going to bed.

151.   INT. HOTEL SUITE NIGHT

FRANK and JOE come in.

                             FRANK
              Was she nice?

                              JOE
              Yeah, she was lovely.

                             FRANK
              What's wrong?

                              JOE
              I miss her.

                             FRANK
              Fucking hell. Everything backfires. You
              can't do fucking anything. (Pause) I'm
              going to be caught.

                    TITLE BOARD: 'Sunday'

152.   INT. CAR DAY

FRANK, JOE and RAY drive back into town. Subdued.

                             FRANK
              Listen. Before we go in, I want to swing
              up by the grave.

111

                              RAY
          Sure.

                              FRANK
                              (To JOE)
          What? Why have you got a puss on
          you about that?

                              JOE
          I don't have a puss on me.

                              FRANK
          You do. Look at you.

Pause. RAY shifts uneasily.

                              FRANK
          It's your mother.

                              JOE
          I just don't do it. I just don't go to the
          grave, Frank. Alright?

                              FRANK
          Yeah. I know you don't. What the fuck
          is that?

                              JOE
          I don't like it.

                              FRANK
          I don't care, you're coming up.

                              JOE
          Jesus. What's wrong with you all of a
          sudden?

                              RAY
          Frank. Go easy.

                              FRANK
          It's his mother. What the hell kind of
          carry-on is that?

                              RAY
          Come on, take it easy.

                              JOE
          It's only a grave.

                              FRANK
          No. It's your mother's grave. It's your
          mother.

JOE

It's not my mother. It's a fuck . . . it's . . .
a hole in the ground.

FRANK

Would you not have have a bit of
fucking respect, no?

JOE
(Almost in tears)
I do have respect, man. She . . . didn't
even know who I was or anything . . .

FRANK

She was sick!

RAY

Here. That's it. I'm not driving yous up
to any fucking grave. You're acting the
bollocks, Frank, whatever the fuck is
wrong with you. Don't take it out on
him. I'm bringing yous home.]

153. EXT. STREET DAY

RAY's car pulls up near the chipper. There is a squad car outside the
chipper.

154. INT. CAR DAY

FRANK, RAY and JOE sit looking at the squad car. None of them knows
what to say or do. A GUARD gets out of the squad car and approaches
them.

RAY
Is there a problem, guard?

GUARD
I'm just going to ask yous to come in,
men.

155. INT. SITTING ROOM DAY

The GUARD brings FRANK, RAY and JOE in. GEORGE and CARMEL sit
with SGT DUGGAN.

FRANK
Is someone going to tell us what this is
about?

113

DUGGAN
I'd just like to have a word with Joe,
Frank. Okay?

FRANK
With Joe? What's wrong?

DUGGAN
I just want to ask him a few questions.

FRANK
What about? Ask me.

DUGGAN
It doesn't have anything to do with
you. Carmel, could you get everyone a
cup of coffee or something?

CARMEL
Yeah, sure.

DUGGAN
Thanks. And if Joe wants to stay here
with me and Mr Beneventi? Alright,
thanks.

FRANK
(On way out)
What's going on?

CARMEL
I'll tell you in a minute.

Now it's just DUGGAN, GEORGE and JOE.

DUGGAN
Do you want to sit down?

JOE sits. GEORGE winks at JOE.

DUGGAN
Okay. The first thing I'm going to ask
you is if you know a girl called Tara
Comisky?

JOE
No.

DUGGAN
No? (Short pause) Because . . . you
were seen with her outside Shadows
nightclub on Wednesday evening.

JOE

Oh okay.

DUGGAN

Do you go to Shadows nightclub?

JOE

I've been there once.

DUGGAN

Last Wednesday?

JOE

Yeah.

DUGGAN

Do you remember the girl?

JOE

Yeah – I didn't know that that was her
second name.

DUGGAN

Okay. Now, I'm here because you have
been accused of raping Tara Comisky.

JOE

What?

DUGGAN

Do you understand what that means?

JOE

I didn't though. I swear to God I didn't.

DUGGAN

Well, now, you see, she hasn't accused
you. A boy called Damien Fitzgibbon
has.

JOE

Damien?

DUGGAN

She was attacked in the graveyard up
near the Grange. And she has
identified Damien as her attacker. [It's
taken us a few days to find him. He's
been staying with his father in
Liverpool.] He said it was you.

JOE

I didn't do it though, you have to ask her.

DUGGAN
She was very drunk. But she
remembers somebody else being
there.

JOE
(Guilt. Self-disappointment)
I didn't know he was raping her. I
thought she was asleep or something.
I didn't know. I just saw them for a
second.

DUGGAN
Okay. But if you were there . . . we
have to eliminate you. You understand
that . . . We need to take a blood test
from you. Okay? Is that okay?

JOE
Yeah.

GEORGE
Good man.

156.   INT. GARDA STATION DAY

GEORGE, FRANK and CARMEL sit in the reception, waiting.

GEORGE
Do you know how I know he didn't do
it? Because he's like us. And we're
thinkers, not doers.

FRANK
He's not capable of it.

GEORGE
That's right.

157.   INT. SAME A LITTLE LATER

FRANK stands reading posters. CARMEL sits with GEORGE, linking his
arm. SGT DUGGAN leads JOE out.

DUGGAN
Now. All done.

GEORGE
Okay, great.

FRANK
Is everything cool?

116

> DUGGAN
> (Regards FRANK coldly)
> I don't think there's . . . anything, for
> him, to worry about. (To JOE:) I think
> you're a bit tired now, are you?

JOE shrugs.

> GEORGE
> Thanks very much.

> DUGGAN
> (To FRANK)
> Could I have a quick word with you for
> a second?

> FRANK
> Yeah. I'll see yous outside in a minute.

There is a confused little pause.

> GEORGE
> (A bit too much of a tone of 'no problem')
> Yeah. Yeah. We'll see you in the car.

158.   INT. INTERVIEW ROOM EVENING

DUGGAN and FRANK come in. He sits casually against a table. She leans
against the wall and offers him a cigarette. They light up.

> DUGGAN
> You didn't hear anything else about
> what we were talking about, did you?
> When we were talking about the
> bookies?

> FRANK
> No. (Short pause) Nothing. (Pause)

> DUGGAN
> Yeah?

> FRANK
> What did I say?

> DUGGAN
> Don't take that tone with me. I'm just
> asking you.

> FRANK
> Yeah, why are you asking me? Are you
> going to humiliate all of us today?

DUGGAN
I'm not trying to humiliate anyone, Frank.
I'm just trying to find out who did it.

FRANK
Fine. Good luck.

DUGGAN
I don't need luck.

FRANK
You want to bet?

DUGGAN
I don't bet.

FRANK
You're right not to. The bookies have
got it all sewn up.

Pause. They look at each other. FRANK leaves. She watches him leave
but doesn't stop him. Then she's alone in the room.

[159. EXT. STREET DAY   ㊺

FRANK stops on the street and looks in the window of a travel agent.]

160.   INT. BEDROOM NIGHT   ㊻

JOE sits in bed. GEORGE knocks and puts his head around the door.

GEORGE
Alright?

JOE
Yeah.

GEORGE comes in and sits on the bed.

GEORGE
All ready for the leaba?

JOE
Yeah.

GEORGE
Are you alright?

JOE
Yeah.

GEORGE
Mad . . .

Pause. They sit there awkwardly. GEORGE picks up the photo of JOE's
mother.

> GEORGE
>
> Did you know . . . your mother was
> partially . . . deaf in one ear?

> JOE
>
> No.

> GEORGE
>
> [Oh yeah. Long as I knew her. Do you
> know how I found out?

> JOE
>
> No.

> GEORGE
>
> I asked her to marry me. When we
> were in the pictures. Leaned over. Said
> it in her ear. And she didn't say
> anything. And I thought 'Oh shit!'
> Because I loved her, you know? And
> she wasn't answering me. But then she
> asked me had I said something? That's
> how I found out.] And then . . . when
> she died . . . they found . . . the doctors
> found a little tooth, in her ear.

> JOE
>
> A tooth?

> GEORGE
>
> A little baby tooth. That when your
> mother was a young girl, they thought
> her tooth fell out and she put it under
> her pillow, and it must've gone in her
> ear. That's what they thought must
> have happened. What do you think of
> that?

JOE smiles, shrugs.

> [GEORGE
>
> She was funny, you know? She would
> have loved that. Something stupid like
> that. She'd have had a laugh at that.]

GEORGE pulls out his wallet, and takes a tiny parcel from the wallet. He
unwraps it. There is nothing there.

119

                           JOE
          Do you have it?

GEORGE looks around a little bit pointlessly.

                        GEORGE
          I think I'm after losing the fucking thing.

                           JOE
          Are you?

They laugh. Pause.

                        GEORGE
          For fuck's sake. Would you believe
          that?

                           JOE
                        (Pause)
          I can't believe Damien dropped me in
          it like that.

                        GEORGE
          That's the way it is though, isn't it?

They sit there.

[161. INT. CHIPPER MORNING   47

CARMEL, GEORGE, FRANK, RAY and JOE sit in the chipper, waiting.
FRANK is dressed to travel, a suitcase at his feet. They drink cups of tea.
Nobody talks. FRANK catches GEORGE's eye. They smile at each other.
CARMEL looks up.

                        CARMEL
          It's here.]

162.   EXT. CHIPPER MORNING   48

They stand on the street. The taxi waits. FRANK embraces CARMEL. She
hugs him tightly.

                        FRANK
          I'll see you soon, yeah? Come out.

                        CARMEL
          Yeah.

FRANK shakes hands with RAY.

                        FRANK
          You keep your nose clean. And
          everything else.

                        RAY
        You know me.

                        FRANK
        Thanks for everything.

                        RAY
        Any time.

FRANK embraces GEORGE.

                        FRANK
        See you Dad.

                        GEORGE
        Look after yourself.

                        FRANK
        I'm going to send a few bob back, you
        get that loan cleared.

                        GEORGE
        Ah no, no. You look after yourself. I'll
        manage.

                        FRANK
        Just shut up, man. I don't know what
        you're like.

FRANK embraces GEORGE again, and turns to JOE. JOE is reluctant to say
goodbye.

                        FRANK
        Come on, man. Say so long.

They shake hands. JOE allows himself to be embraced.

                        FRANK
        You mind yourself. And who you pick
        up with. (Whispers:) There's a bag
        behind the brick.

FRANK embraces CARMEL again. [SGT DUGGAN pulls up in a squad car
driven by a guard. She rolls down the window. FRANK is pissed off. He
moves away from the others. He leans on her car, a picture of jaded
tolerance.

                        DUGGAN
        Are you away somewhere Frank?

                        FRANK
        Yeah.

> DUGGAN
>
> It wouldn't be Chicago, by any chance
> would it?

> FRANK
>
> You're psychic.

> DUGGAN
>
> No. I'm just not stupid.

> FRANK
>
> Never said you were. You cleared the
> boy.

> DUGGAN
>
> Pity I didn't have more time to spend
> on this brother.

> FRANK
>   (ie, 'Don't torture yourself')
> Maybe not.

> DUGGAN
>
> My problem is that I can't make up my
> mind about you.

> FRANK
>
> Do you know why that is? It's because
> I'm just ordinary.

DUGGAN gives him a look of 'Who do you think you're fooling?' She rolls up her window and drives away.] FRANK winks at his family and gets in the taxi. They watch him go. GEORGE, CARMEL and RAY go into the chipper. JOE lingers on the street.

163.   EXT. COAST DAY

JOE cycles along the coast.

164.   EXT. GIRLS SCHOOL DAY   ㊾

GIRLS pour out of school at home time. JOE is waiting on his bike. He sees TARA, and cycles up to her. JOE and TARA stand there for a moment. [We spin around them in a frantic circle.]

END.

Notes on Postproduction

The perceived wisdom is that each page in a movie's shooting script represents one minute of screen time. The script for Saltwater was 84 pages long. So when we put the film all together as per the script there was a bit of a panic for a few days. The film was three hours long, not 84 minutes.

It was baffling. 'But this shouldn't be,' we said, looking at each other. Now had the film been made for a studio with a lot of money behind it things could have gone either way. They could either say, 'Get this monster into reasonable shape or you're fired,' or more unlikely – 'It works! Let's get behind this baby and make it the surprise hit of the summer.'

But our film wasn't made with a big studio behind it. We made it for the low-low price of £2 million. We had no distribution in place. It was an independent film backed by the BBC, the Irish film board, RTE, and a Spanish pre-sale to Alta films. We didn't just need to sell the finished product to the public but to distributors in countries all over the world in order to reach the public.

Several factors would govern our ability to find distribution. Does it work? Does the distributor like it? Are there any recognisable stars? But most importantly, can the distributor sell it? To stay in business the distributor needs to convince the exhibitors (i.e. cinema owners) that people will come to watch it. And this really means a lot of people. And this is where the length of the film becomes an issue – a three-hour movie can only be shown half as many times in a day as a 90-minute one.

Contractually therefore, I had to deliver a film no more than 100 minutes long. These notes tell the story scene by scene of how we attack the movie's length while trying to retain the story and sense we'd worked so hard to achieve during the seven week shoot.

1

Scene 3   The card game

Emer, the film's editor, probably spent more time on this scene than any other, trying to pull it down into some kind of manageable shape. As shot it was simply too long as an opening scene. The audience might start to go, 'Is this it? – A film about a family playing cards?' It needed to reach its climax faster. At least ten times we pulled this scene out of the cut altogether. But as we struggled with the first half hour of the film and dropped more and more scenes we increasingly felt the card game gave a coherence to the characters – they had a relationship. This was always its function in the script anyhow.

Whenever Emer became bored or tired of working on some other part of the film she'd go, 'Will we have a crack at the card game?' It took a day to shoot and I got loads and loads of takes of everybody which gave us the freedom to play around with it in postproduction. The actors must have done the scene forty times by the end of the day. Everybody nearly went bonkers. Except for Conor Mullen who cleverly was really drinking the beer that was replaced in front of him at the beginning of each take. He looked at me at lunchtime and said, 'I'm buckled.' By eight o'clock everybody was drinking it.

2

Scene 11   Frank smoking alone

We moved this scene from Monday morning in the script to Tuesday evening in the film, where it became part of a montage to give the story a bit of a breather. It showed me that an old adage is true – if you film an actor doing nothing their context inflects their performance. Doing nothing on Monday morning he looks bored, doing nothing on Tuesday evening he looks like he's planning something.

3

Scenes 18-26

It's still a little shocking how much we shot which just isn't in the film at all. The film was too long, but where? Everywhere? Was it a case of trying to keep bits of everything or just to forget about entire sequences? It was hard to know. I'd shot a lot of material improvised or written just before going into production. And in many cases this stuff was working better than stuff shot according to the approved shooting script. We liked each scene as it stood, but placed altogether there was just too much going on. Emer suggested we start at the beginning and take out anything which wasn't absolutely necessary and see what happened. For instance was it essential to set so many things up? Frank on the bus berating the young mother and then speaking about his family in the Manpower office were two of the best scenes Peter McDonald had in the whole assembly, but how much did we need to know about him for his character to work? Equally where the fight at the school and Damien urging Joe to look at Miss Brosnan's breasts served to *bring* the two boys together, wasn't it enough just to *see* them together? To Show rather than Tell . . .

And again Frank's scenes with Lisa at the repossessed truck and with George at the broken down car. They showed Simon McCurdie's grip on the town, but didn't we show that again later? How many times do we need to convey a piece of information? But at the same time these scenes were steeped in character. Emer's favourite scene was Frank and George at the car, and here we were cutting it out! It was confusing because we liked spending time with the characters but were we starving the audience of incident? The main objective was to pull the length down to 100 minutes or under so we became merciless, and slowly we became confident that we were giving information in an interesting way, and keeping the pace leisurely too. But now we're telling in nine minutes what had taken 40 in the first assembly of scenes. We'd found a direction, the right one? We couldn't be sure this early so we just ploughed on.

4

Scene 28   Joe and Damien smoking

Shot, not used.

5

Scene 30   Ray avoiding Deborah in the bar

Shot, not used. This was a pretty cool scene done in one shot. It was shot in a GAA club in Cabra whose bar was on two levels. A pool table was on the lower level. We shot it from the upper level. We opened on the pool balls breaking and moved to take Deborah coming in talking with her friends. As she comes up the stairs the camera passes Ray's face quickly and we just catch him reacting to Deborah's voice behind him. The camera keeps following her until she sits in a booth and we keep moving to reveal Ray's drink and his cigarette left smoking in the ashtray. Ray himself has vanished.

It took a while to rehearse this shot. We had a lot of extras to coordinate and it was difficult to get Ray's reaction to Deborah's voice timed right. Finally after the focus puller and camera operator felt they had the move timed as well as they could we went for a take. We just needed someone to break the pool balls. Our producer, Rob Walpole, was with me every day on set. We were *always* behind, always losing time, but we were having an absolute blast. It was rare for us not to be having a laugh. But this day we had to get out of the location so Rob steps up to the plate, all serious, 'I'll break the balls first time, let's get this shot and let's get out of here.'

So last focus checks, checks on the actors, 'Everyone settle,' says Peter Agnew our First A.D. I sit at the monitor watching this triangle of pool balls that are about to burst apart, plunging the scene into action, all in one perfect shot. 'Standby.' 'Quiet please!' 'Settle!' 'Rolling!' 'Speed!' 'Mark it.' 'Thirty. Take One.' I nod to the First. 'Action!' he shouts.

The cue ball rolls slowly into frame and continues, slowing down, past all the other balls, and comes to a feeble halt on the back cushion. He didn't even touch one. The scene swings into action anyway while Peter Agnew tries to call a halt and get everyone back to first positions. I wander over to the banister and look down to see the pool shark, Mister Efficient Let's Get This In One Walpole lying across the table, hiding his head while his body shakes with laughter. We finally got it after seven takes, Rob hit them each time, but we just could never find anywhere to put this scene now that the configuration was changing. We tried it all over the place and it didn't fit any more. The rhythm of the script was by now different to the rhythm of the film.

6

Scene 34   Joe and Damien cycle away
Dialogue changed on the day to:

DAMIEN. Split up!
JOE. What?
DAMIEN. Split up!

7

Scene 36   George asks Frank for money
We cut out the bit where George tries to pour himself a drink of whiskey. We felt that heavy drinking might negate the character. It might feel like he's in trouble *because* he drinks rather than the other way round. We decided to make him a more together person so as to make Simon's takeover appear more aggressive. I took out the detail of the whiskey in scene nine for this reason too.

8

Scene 37   George and Frank arrive at the bookies
In the script the clerk behind the counter is a man. I changed the part to a woman and made up this dialogue for her:

GEORGE. Orla . . .
ORLA. I'm not going to the pictures with you.
GEORGE. Ahwww . . . Is he in?

9

Scene 38   Frank and George ask Simon for a break in the loan
As written this scene was colossal. It was about twelve minutes or something. Because we'd cut and trimmed everything up to here so far this one just felt wrong.

So lots of it was chopped. It was a pity to lose the stuff with the calendar and Simon on the phone at the beginning as this was some of the funniest and most idiosyncratic material we had.

10

Scene 39   Frank and George fight in the chipshop

We chopped out George's explanation about their mother's insurance policy and how upset he was when she died. By now we were in a flow, resigned to keeping things shorter than they'd been shot, and this information seemed unnecessary. I don't say any of this in a negative or regretful way. All this cutting was a positive and ultimately creative process. It was a great challenge. It helped that I'd so much extra material than was simply on the page. The scene as shot was pretty much made up on the day.

GEORGE. You couldn't just give me that twelve quid, now look.
FRANK. I am not the clown who borrowed the money from him in the first place!

11

Scene 40   Ray lectures

Again we shot all of this but cut most of it. The students were discovered using a long crane shot while Ray spoke. Crane shots tended to be cut because of their unity of movement. If a scene was shot in one long crane move, well then the scene is really as long as the shot. Emer had warned me about this during the first week of the shoot, urging me to get cover shots. I did and this is precisely why we were able to get out of a lot of trouble while editing. We were never really constrained by a lack of cover.

For this reason I'd tell first-time directors to take their editor's advice while shooting. The editor is always urging you to give yourself more options. Sometimes their demands may seem unreasonable. After a particularly gruelling piece of filming your editor will probably say 'Why didn't you get . . . X shot?' And often I felt frustrated during the shoot when Emer suggested more shots or re-shoots. I complied as best I could given the limited time. But I was glad I did.

Sometimes when directing a scene you may do a wide shot or two shot where the performances are great and you think that everything looks cool and you don't want anything else. Believe me, this is not a decision to be made on the day. Get more. You don't have to use it if indeed you do have your perfect master. But you just might get yourself out of a few wobblies in post. A scene mightn't seem as great to you six months after you've shot it without the atmosphere that was on set that day. Use all the time you have. Five minutes at the end of the day? – Stick another lens on, shoot it again. You've nothing to lose.

This is where first-time directors need to learn about the politics between the crew and director. While you've got to be friendly in order to have a reasonable time, you've got to try and get what you want. Sometimes a person will come up to you, probably your First A.D., and say, 'It'd be great for morale if we could finish a bit earlier tonight. We went a bit over last night.' My advice is this, remember, no film has ever been made famous by its easy shoot. Get what you need.

12

Scene 41A   Ray and Deborah in the office
The scenes between Ray and Deborah and Ray and Carmel were all mostly improvised. This scene was improvised in rehearsals with me trying to write something better than the shit I had. As written the scenes with Deborah weren't very interesting. She's just like this Monica Lewinsky character in the previous script.

We had a good laugh coming up with these new scenes. The speech patterns strike me as very real. They don't seem 'written.' Of course this is down to great acting from Conor Mullen and Eva Birthistle. But as the director, I reluctantly claim the credit. Thank you.

13

Scene 42   Joe plays rifle game
This was a sweet little atmospheric scene. Again it was one which just seemed out of place in the new scheme of things. And we never found anywhere else to put it.

14

Scene 48-54   Montage – Tuesday night into Wednesday morning
The initial scene here, where Joe was having a wank, was something Laurence Kinlan was very excited about. He went around the whole crew trying to get them to come down and watch it. He was so popular with everybody we ran into difficulties. We could never find him. He'd disappear before his scenes. Everyone would have to run around looking for him. When he was found he'd be completely oblivious. There he'd be, standing in the back of the electrical truck or somewhere, talking to one of the drivers. They'd bring him down to the set and he'd blink at me and say 'What scene are we doing? Do I have many lines?'

He had a beautiful quality. He was sixteen and he never questioned anything we were doing. It was better never to direct him. He was pure instinct and if you fooled around with what he was doing he suddenly looked like he was acting. I was amazed by his natural ability and often all I could do was shake my head and say, 'He has no idea what he's doing and neither do I.' We cut out the wanking bit and just used the shot of Frank from the top of the scene to kick off the montage.

Again I cut the whiskey drinking out of George's bit, and just suggested that Brian Cox study his shoe instead, as if he's miles away.

I don't know why I didn't get Conor and Eva to make love in Scene 51 as scripted. I shot this on only my second day and maybe I was too embarrassed? But it just felt like more of a betrayal to me to have Ray simply lying there with Deborah. You know, that he wasn't just looking for sex, that he was fundamentally lonely. Actually, thinking about it now, I can't have been too embarrassed. We spent most of that day shooting sex scenes for a different part (Scene 122).

The music for this montage was The Plague Monkeys. I hired them to do the score after I heard their first album, *Surface Tension*. I was after its gentle percussive feeling. And Carol Keogh's voice is as original and beautiful as any singer you'd care to mention. I loved all the bells and sounds you couldn't really identify which were samples from everyday ambience.

At the beginning of the process we got off to a shaky start. The band were trying to give me a 'film soundtrack' with a 'scary bit', a 'fast bit, a 'tense bit' in a generic sort of way. They'd never done anything like this before and what they were giving me was all a bit literal. But as they became more aware that it was *their* sound I was after, their pared-down style, it got much better.

What they composed for the above montage came about by accident. I was at one of their concerts at Vicar Street in Dublin and I heard them play a new song. It was really short, just one verse and one chorus. It struck me as by far the best song of the night. When I asked about it later they were a bit dismissive. It was just something they'd started messing about with in rehearsals. It didn't even have its own title. They called it *Seachange Part 2* because it reminded them of another song. I asked them to record it for me. And when I heard a rough demo I knew it had to go in the film. A few weeks later, recording the score, Donal O'Mahoney, their guitarist, played me a gentle 'Italian version' he'd been working on at home. I put it over the montage and I just thought, 'This looks like a film.' This montage with their music is still one of my favourite bits in *Saltwater*. The band recorded a version of *Seachange Part 2* for our end credits and it's also on their second album, *The Sunburn Index* (Track 4).

15

Scenes 57-63   Ray gets up – and goes to get a cure

We shot all this stuff. I remember the lighting for Scene 57 took ages, and the scene lasts about five seconds, and we still cut it! Cillian Murphy played the barman in Scene 62 and it was a pretty funny scene. The scene where Ray gets sick in the toilets was, bizarrely, one of the most beautiful in the film. The light was cold and relentless, the only warmth was the red in Ray's face. We improvised that after he's puked, he rehearses being 'normal.' He pretends to talk to someone in the mirror. 'Really?' he went, 'Wow, that's . . . ', he adopted a serious face, 'That's . . .

amazing . . . ' We had to be ruthless to chop all this out. It hurt Emer especially to lose Cillian Murphy because, as she'd say adopting a grave 'accept Jesus into your life' expression, 'He's absolutely gorgeous. He's a ride!'

16

Scene 66   Damien and Joe in Damien's house

We shot all this but only used the very top of the scene to establish that Joe was mitching off school for the afternoon. We cut all the rest. It took ages to shoot. All the pond stuff and the dog getting hit with the toast and everything. Lots of us kept having a go and kept missing him. Luke Quigley Snr finally hit him and we got the reaction we wanted. It didn't hurt, it was only a piece of toast. But it took ages, and we still cut it all out. And ironically for me this scene is the crux of Joe's story. Here he is in an alien environment, uncomprehending what he sees. But he doesn't leave. It's one of those moments where you're not a child but not really a grown-up either. The scene was also (heavily) hinting at Damien's weird upbringing – is his relationship with his mother sexual? This was also David O'Rourke's best scene in the film. He was only fifteen and very embarrassed at some of the things he had to do.

This was easily the maddest scene in the film and it was all fast and exciting but in the context of the film it's all essentially back story. It looks like an attempt to explain Damien rather than just show him as he is.

17

Scene 67   Damien asks Joe to go to Shadows

Again we cut this because we were telling the audience that Joe Is Going To Go To A Bad Place when in fact all we have to do is show him there by opening on the fight outside Shadows (Scene 72). The audience get in a second what would have taken us two minutes to do. Simply, Joe Is In A Bad Place.

18

Scene 68   Carmel catches Frank rehearsing the robbery

We changed the dialogue at the end of the scene on the day:

CARMEL. So. You're having a bit of a play. In your room, are you?
FRANK. You know yourself.
CARMEL. I'll see you later.
FRANK. Thanks again, Carmel.

19

Scene 69   The woman and child on the beach. Larry falls in the water
We shot this but it never made the cut. For me it was just town colour. The woman
and child were from the bus scene earlier (Scene 19) and we knew Larry, the town
drinker from earlier scenes too (Scenes 27 and 44). It wasn't supposed to mean
anything it was just to evoke a sense of place. The third take was the best because
the baby was playing in the sand and his mother was talking gently to him. As he
tentatively got to his feet to show her a bit of seaweed, Larry fell into the sea. We
shot it at dusk and the light was beautiful. I fought and fought to keep the scene
in, but without the bus scene to establish the mother and child earlier it just seemed
confusing. According to everybody. Not me. (Incidentally, here's a tip about making a small toddler cry on cue in a film. If you give them chocolate and then take
it away for a few seconds you get perfect crying on cue which stops immediately
when you give the chocolate back. It's very humane – on film the child's distress
will always appear greater, because we project the worst.)

20

Scene 70   Joe puts aftershave on
We shot this and didn't use it.

21

Scene 71   Ray and Carmel in the bar
I wrote, or re-wrote this scene with Conor Mullen and Valerie Spelman about ten
minutes before we shot it. Conor Mullen is one of the most honest people I've ever
met. If something's bothering him he says it. Most people assume that if they're
uncomfortable doing something, it's their fault, 'Oh, it must be me, I mustn't
understand this yet.' But Conor just comes straight out with his doubts. In one way
I feel 'Oh God I'm going to have to bluff my way through this,' when he confronts
me, but in another way I felt, 'This is refreshing. Let's look at this and question
what we're doing for a minute.' And I believe every frame of Conor's performance
because he's comfortable with what he's doing. Because he's questioned everything
to the point where he's gone through a process of learning to trust every decision
he's made. And he looks real.

22

Scene 74   Joe and Damien in the nightclub
Shot. Not used.

23

Scene 74   Joe meets Tara

The bit with the bouncer was cut out. Tara comes up to Joe in the film and asks 'What's your name?' which is in fact the last thing she asks him in the scene. It just seemed like a better opening line so we changed it in the cut.

24

Scene 77   Joe and Tara get beaten up

This is one of my favourite scenes. It feels very real to me. The camera operation by Cian be Buitlear is great, it's all hand-held and constantly moving. We used one or two out of focus shots to give it more of an immediate feel. Cian started out doing documentaries. I asked him about keeping things coherent in hand-held mode. He said, 'When you're making documentaries and you're trying to catch someone or something on the move, you're just constantly walking backwards. It's just something you get used to, finding composition where you can. And in a drama with a choreographed fight, you've got your marks on the ground so you can suddenly move from one mark to another while the focus puller keeps it sharp.'

The actor playing Junior, Mark Dunne, insisted that Caroline O'Boyle, playing Tara, actually hit him for real. Caroline was very cool, very calm. She was seventeen, had never been in a film before and was pretty much up for anything. She thumped him across the face in every take. And every time he 'hit' her she fell perfectly. One time Cian moved in behind her and she fell on top of him and the camera, but no-one was hurt and we kept going.

In the script Joe and Tara manage to escape from Junior's gang. In the film they're beaten until they're completely submissive.

25

Scene 78   Joe and Tara sitting at the beach

Pat Doyle was our boom operator. All the way through the shoot he kept giving me ideas. Before we went into production Emer said to me, 'When you start shooting you'll notice a tension between the sound department and the camera department. The camera operator will always be telling the boom operator that his microphone is too close and it's going to be in shot. The boom operator is going to try and get as close to the actors as he can. I'm going to give you a piece of advice. Fight for the sound guys. The temptation will always be to get your picture and tidy up the sound in post with ADR (additional dialogue recording). You've got to resist that temptation because an actor's performance in ADR is never as good as the performance on the day. It's not even 40 per cent as good. You can hear it. It sounds funny. It's the actor's voice but it doesn't sound like it's coming from their body. And you don't want a film that looks dubbed.'

So I took her advice and always tried to get the sound department what they needed. Sometimes they'd simply need to record the atmosphere in a room after we'd finished shooting. (I know this seems weird but when you're doing the sound mix you can't just have the actors speaking in a vacuum. There's ambient sound around us all the time.) And this meant getting the whole crew, inside and out, to stay still, turn off all generators and engines and be silent. It was always a lovely moment after a scene. Like a moment of prayer or something with everyone standing still with their heads bowed so as not to catch anyone's eye and start laughing. And Pat would stand there, earphones on his head, just recording the air.

And because I was fighting their corner I think Pat felt quite relaxed and would chip in with ideas which I took and usually used. An example would be Joe's constant reaction to something bad as 'Fucking hell,' which sounded so funny the way Laurence said it. The first instance of this was in this scene where Pat suggested I change the line 'My fucking heart' to 'fucking hell'. Ironically, we did re-record this whole scene because of all the industrial noise coming across the water at the Bull Wall in Dollymount where we shot it. But I used the original recording we did on the day, industrial noises and all, because Emer was right. The original was immeasurably better than the ADR.

26

Scene 81   Joe sees Damien and Tara in the graveyard
We had to reshoot the rape. When we looked at the rushes it was hard to make out what was going on. This was for a number of reasons. Firstly, David O'Rourke was nervous about doing it and I was equally uncomfortable trying to persuade him. Caroline O'Boyle as usual was taking everything in her stride and didn't care what she did or what anyone else did. We were right down to the wire with only a tiny amount of time to do it, and with the pressure on I lost my nerve. Emer had come out to the location in Lusk. With the last few minutes of shooting, people were packing up and going home. She came up to me and said, 'Conor, you don't have it. You've got to get his pants down and really go for it.' I stood there with my hand on a gravestone, scratching at the moss and, almost tearful with exhaustion and tension, I turned on her. 'I can't: I just can't, alright?!' And we wrapped. Of course she was right, so on the last day of the shoot (the fight outside Shadows) we built a black tent. Peter McDonald put on David's costume. Neither he nor Caroline shied away from the task and we had it.

27

Scene 83   Joe in the bathroom
In the film Joe nurses his torn ear. I don't think we had a toilet.

Scene 84 *Joe in bedroom*

We used the second half of this scene to show Joe waking up from a nightmare and holding his mum's photo and we moved it to just after Scene 111.

Scene 87 *Frank and George in the chipper*

We shot this but didn't use it. I thought it was a beautiful scene, as did Oliver Curtis, our director of photography. It started tight on Frank filling salt-cellars at a table. And then he just stops and we track back slowly to reveal George sitting at another table reading the paper. And we keep pulling back until we see the whole chipshop and these two figures sitting there with no business, doing nothing, not talking to each other after their fight. And then Frank gets up, untying his apron, to go and prepare for the robbery. It was a great scene, but it took two minutes to tell the story in silence and it was much more immediate to simply cut to Frank getting his stuff ready.

30

Scene 93 *Frank robs the bookies*

This took a day to shoot. It was really hard because there was just so much to cover. We were shooting in a new studio which wasn't really soundproof. It was beside a railway track and near the airport. We kept having to stop because of noise. Also, in a studio next door sets were being built for another film and we could hear them.

The lights on the enclosed set for the bookies made the heat unbearable. Peter McDonald was in a Parka jacket and a balaclava all day and Brendan Gleeson was in a heavy wool suit. Tempers were very frayed. As usual I was trying to get the best sound I could and I was continually asking the actors not to 'do' stuff which was out of shot, and this was curtailing their performances. There was a bit of a blow-up and then we continued. It was a day everybody was glad to see the back of.

But we got great stuff. Brendan Gleeson's little ad libs are inspired: as he hands the envelopes to Peter McDonald, 'Some of them's not money now, they're only dockets. They'll only be weighing you down.' As he takes off his shirt, he looks down at his clerk, Orla, imploring her not to watch him undress: 'For fuck's sake, Orla, give us a break, would ya?'

The ad libbing at the top of the scene between Simon and Charlie (Alan King):

SIMON. What the fuck does that spell?
CHARLIE. Xylophone.
SIMON. But it doesn't fit, sure! What's the clue?
CHARLIE. 17 down, musical instrument. Begins with Z.

SIMON. Zither! Zither! Zither!
CHARLIE. What the fuck's a zither?

31

Scenes 94-103   The chase

This was a saga. We shot the first part on a cloudy day. The problem was that the initial shot of Frank leaving Simon on the street was shot in bright sunlight. Emer was imploring me to shoot the first half again in bright weather to match Frank's initial departure.

Rob Walpole used to pick me up every morning, as we lived near each other. It was great having the producer on set at all times. He could have rows with people I was unhappy with, without me getting involved. He was someone I could confide in and check things with as I learned the ropes. He always urged me to get as much or as little as I wanted.

We were driving up to Skerries one morning at about 6.30 am and I saw the sun begin to break through the clouds. We decided to dump the day's schedule and reshoot the chase.

We were already way behind due to loads of cock-ups (eg, the camera truck and electrical truck showing up at different locations). But the chase was important so it was worth making it look good. So we split the crew up. I took the second unit camera crew (Cian de Buitlear, Donal Gilligan) and Rob took the first (Oliver Curtis, Ciaran Kavanagh). He would supervise reshoots of what we'd already done, while I worked out and shot the second half of the chase. It was a mad day. We were trading actors over the radio. 'How long until Pete's free?'

'Another ten minutes.'

'Can we have Alan?'

'Yeah, but we need him straight back.'

Pete (Frank), Alan (Charlie) and Laurence (Joe) were all doing their own stunts. They were wrecked, running around, jumping over walls, falling into and off bicycles, it's a wonder no-one broke their leg.

It was hectic but we got it. The last shot was again a suggestion by Pat Doyle. As Pete ran out of the lane in one of the takes, a load of money fell out of his pocket and blew across the road. It's the take we used in the film and Pete's reaction as he looks at it and continues up the street is real – he's expecting someone to call cut. But it looked so good we kept filming. And Pat's suggestion was that Laurence, as he walks away collecting himself, should see some money on the ground and surreptitiously pick it up and put it in his pocket. It was a great suggestion and a perfect way to end the sequence. And it took advantage of our fortunate mistake.

As the sun was setting I moved off down the beach to shoot the 8 mm footage of Maria Beneventi (Deirdre O'Kane) which makes up the bulk of Joe's dreams. Where Rob was filming was practically hidden from the sun by now. But he still needed one shot, Charlie jumping over the wall and tumbling across the sand.

The crew were saying 'The light's gone, Rob, you won't get it.' This was at 7.55 pm and the crew were supposed to wrap at 8.00 pm. The sun was behind a low cloud on the horizon. Rob said, 'Let's just give it till eight.'

'It's gone, Rob.' Everyone was beginning to pack up.

'Just have Alan ready,' Rob goes, 'If it's still dark at eight we'll leave.'

So Alan sat at the top of the wall and Oliver, Ciaran the focus-puller, Howard the steadicam operator, James the gaffer, Davy the best boy, and Rob all stood staring into the sky and at bang on 8.00 pm the sun burst through the cloud and blazed for thirty seconds. 'Standby!' 'Rolling!' 'Speed!' 'Mark it!' 'Set!' 'Action'!' And Rob got his shot. Now I wasn't there, but I know how competitive Rob is and I can just see him strutting around, vindicated. It was a great moment of triumph, like somebody up there liked us, and it was a good omen.

So Rob came around to the beach where we had the 8 mm camera and while everybody went home, me, Cian, Donal Gilligan and Rob took turns banging off a roll of film as Deirdre walked across the sand, the low evening sun behind her. It's a day we remember fondly. The 8 mm film had to be sent off to Germany to be developed so I had no idea what we'd gotten until three weeks later when Emer rang me up and said, 'It's magical.'

32

Scene 104   Joe comes into the yard

We shot this and didn't use it as it broke the tension. It's the difference between seeing Joe come home and knocking on the bedroom door, and having Frank and Ray standing in the bedroom . . . and there's a knock at the door.

33

Scene 106   Frank decides to open door

Most of this was ad libbed. Ray hitting Frank, for example.

34

Scene 108   The three boys in the bedroom

We gave the line 'It must be thirty grand' to Ray on the day. It was funnier to have Frank surprised at his haul.

35

Scenes 109-110   Driving by the bookies. The debate on the pier

Both these scenes were shot but unused. Rather than reflect on what happened, which is probably a writer's instinct not a director's, it seemed better just to move ahead with the story.

36

Scene 112   Frank and Joe in their beds at dawn

This was a really nice scene but again the above applies.

I asked Emer recently about our process of cutting the film down and were we asking the right questions? She said, 'You know, it's weird, the trend is now that films are getting longer and longer.' But we've all sat through shit dialogue waiting for the next 'good bit' and if you feel that the audience might begin to shift and stir at a certain moment you've got to question it. We went through a process and we made our decisions. That's what postproduction is for and whether we were asking the right questions or not doesn't matter any more. I believe that the film is good. But the niggling thing always there is that I've seen all the stuff the audience haven't. And maybe, unconsciously, I think they're still there?

37

Scene 114   Sgt Duggan interrogates Frank in the chipper

Again this was a long scene which Emer dug into and pulled the essence out to make a shorter coherent version. Frank throwing the cigarettes and lighter over the page 3 model's breasts was a weird thing for me. For weeks I was being shown more and more page 3 models, with the art department asking me which one I wanted. For some reason I couldn't make up my mind. I needed to see more.

38

Scene 117   The academics' reception

Only the very end of this scene is missing from the film – where Ray goes over to Deborah to ask her if she'll come away for a chat. There was a really good take where Conor Mullen accidentally banged into Eva Birthistle's arm. She was sipping some wine and he knocked her glass into her teeth with a 'thwak'. Her wine spilled and Conor didn't even notice, he was scanning the room to see if Ray was being 'watched' by anyone. He just carried on regardless. If this bit of the scene had made the cut, I would have used this take. It was brilliant.

39

Scene 118   Ray and Deborah in the student bar

Again, like Scene 41A, I wrote this scene in rehearsals improvising with Conor and Eva as the original I'd written was crap.

40

Scenes 122-133

And again I can't believe we shot all this stuff and didn't use it. And as an action sequence with stunt men and fights and smashing a car up, naturally it took forever to shoot. This was the biggest decision we made in the cut. You'll notice that at a certain point in the film Ray's windshield is cracked. The reasons for this are in these deleted scenes. Hugh O'Connor, playing Vyvian, flew over from England to do these scenes. He was working on another film. Hugh. What can I say? I owe you many drinks.

41

Scene 136 Frank talking to the town drinkers, Larry and Mack
This was a funny scene with a pratfall introduced on the day. As Larry (played by Billy Roche, the best playwright in Ireland) goes to the toilet he feints a punch at Mack and walks out of shot. Mack (Eamonn Hunt) stands there for a second and then collapses.

42

Scene 140 Ray driving to lecture
We shot this with Ray improvising his questions to Konigsberg. It was really good but we caught the whole crew on the low loader reflected in the windows as we drove along.

43

Scenes 149-152
Again, all shot and never used. It was all good but because the rest of the cut was working out at a faster pace, everything just seemed to sit down here. The corridor drunk scene was especially good. We farted around in the cut, pulling various bits and pieces out, but finally I decided we just go straight from Frank and Ray watching Joe dance to them pulling up at home with the police there. And it just worked.

44

Scene 155 Duggan questions Joe
The worst line in the script is here. 'It's taken us a few days to find him. He's been staying with his father in Liverpool.' I wouldn't even shoot it on the day. And Gina Moxley wouldn't have said it.

45

Scene 159 Frank looks in the window of a travel agent
Shot. Not used. Without this scene the ending is fairly ambiguous. People have asked afterwards, 'Where's he going?' I say, in the context of the film, not the script, 'Probably America.' But that's what I intended to show, but haven't. When I ask

people, 'Where do you think he's going?' the answers are terrifyingly varied. 'Prison.' 'Italy.' 'He's joining the police.'

That he's leaving by taxi shows he's leaving of his own free will. And the fact that he tells his father he's going to send him money shows that he's going somewhere either to work or pretend to work while he lives off the money he's stolen.

Having said all this though, why leave out the detail of the travel agent? I think it was because it signalled the ending too heavily. There was just something *too* neat about it. I suppose it's a matter of taste and temperament. And we had the freedom to follow our instincts because our budget was so low.

Were we making a film with a budget of say £10 million or more as opposed to the £2 million we had, the input of our financiers would probably have been much greater. And this is the irony – a lower budget can give a first-time director more freedom than constraint in postproduction. Time is limited and decisions have to be made over a matter of two and a half months. And those decisions are more than likely going to be made by the director and the editor because so few other people are on the limited payroll. I spoke to a film director recently who had shot a film for about £15 million. His postproduction process became seemingly endless because so many people had a legitimate right to criticise the cut, demand changes, and even suggest reshooting scenes months after principal photography was completed. This director told me at one point that he added up all the people he was answerable to. All in all, between heads of production companies and executives, he was expected to listen to and give time to sixteen critical voices at any one time. And these were people ringing from all over the world, so he was talking to people at all hours of the day and night. It was an exhausting experience. Sixteen opinions at any one time! The luxury that Emer and I had was that where executives for a studio may try to shore up what they see as holes in the plot, we were able to actively try to create holes and make some space and hopefully allow the audience to make up their own minds as to aspects of the story.

46

Scene 160   George tells Joe about his mother's tooth
We cut out the bit where George talks about proposing to his wife. There was nothing wrong with it except that it just makes the scene feel longer than it should.

I think this scene has an unusual effect in the story. Without really resolving anything it just has an atmosphere of resolution. There's a gentle winding down and the tooth disappearing is an unexpected laugh where we mightn't have felt there was a place for one. I'm really pleased with this work but I'm not sure I can explain its effect. Perhaps it's like a tiny connection to the spirit world for Joe and George, a suggestion of their mortality which binds them to Maria finally even though they've been anxious to avoid talking about her before. I think this scene somehow provides a sense of perspective. We just know we're coming to the end of the story.

139

We changed the last lines of dialogue on the day to:

JOE. Dad. Were you always a bit mad?
GEORGE. A bit. Always. You'll go mad too. Sleep tight.

47

Scene 161   They all sit waiting for the taxi
We shot this and didn't use it.

48

Scene 162   Frank's farewell
We shot the stuff between Frank and Sgt Duggan but felt it repetitive and unnecessary. Gina Moxley, playing Duggan even said to me, 'You'll probably never use this!' She was right. Again, it was just too neat for my taste.

49

Scene 164   Joe goes to Tara's school
We didn't have time to 'spin around them' as per the script. It was the old story, a shot like that would have taken too long to organise. This was the final week of the shoot and we were still behind. However, I knew this was the last shot in the film and I wanted it to look like *something*. So we used a crane and a camera with variable speeds. As we crane down towards Laurence crossing the road with his bike, we speed up the camera and so everything goes into slow motion. There was no wind and we wanted Caroline O'Boyle's hair to blow a little bit as she stepped into shot so one of the props guys stood there with an electric fan. It didn't blow a lot, just a bit, but it's a nice effect. The seventh take was the best one because the schoolgirls cross the camera at the perfect time.

And that was it. I owe so much to Emer Reynolds for helping, saving, me with my three-hour extravaganza. I think we did the business. I'm proud of what we did and I hope she is too.

Things worked out well. We screened the film in Berlin at the 2000 Festival and as I write this we've sold *Saltwater* in 15 territories around the world so far.

Conor McPherson, Dublin, August 2000

Above: Peter McDonald as Frank. Below: Laurence Kinlan as Joe

Above: Brian Cox as George and Peter McDonald as Frank playing cards
Below: Brendan Gleeson (centre) as Simple Simon and Alan King (right) as Charlie
pay a visit to Brian Cox as George

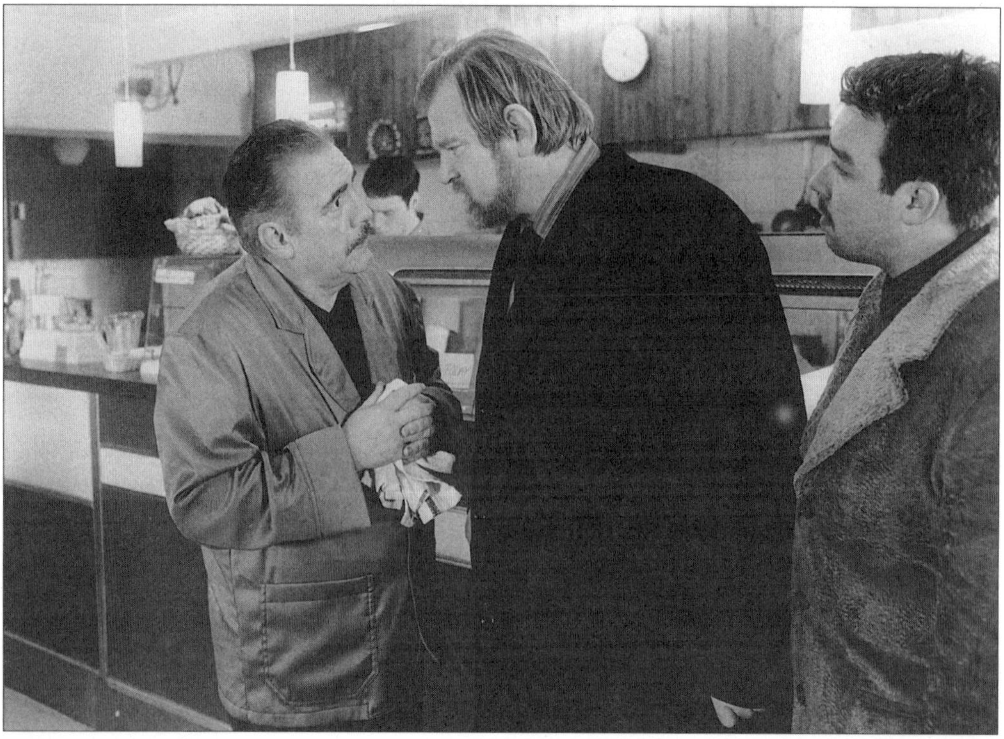

Above: Peter McDonald as Frank and Brendan Gleeson as Simple Simon
Below: Conor Mullen as Ray stands up to ask his question

SALTWATER

Cast

FRANK	Peter McDonald
GEORGE	Brian Cox
RAY	Conor Mullen
JOE	Laurence Kinlan
SIMPLE SIMON	Brendan Gleeson
CARMEL	Valerie Spelman
DEBORAH McCEEVER	Eva Birthistle
DAMIEN	David O'Rourke
CHARLIE	Alan King
TARA	Caroline O'Boyle
SGT DUGGAN	Gina Moxley
LARRY (OLD MAN)	Billy Roche
DUIGNAN	Simon Jewel
LAWLESS	Sean O'Flanagan
ROONEY	Peter Coonan
MR FANNING	Pat Shortt
BOUNCER ONE / TONY	Anto Nolan
HENNESSY	Ciaran Delaney
JOHN TRAYNOR	Michael McElhatton
BOUNCER TWO / DARREN	Simon Delaney
ORLA	Lisa Tierney Keogh
TONY REGAN	Garrett Keogh
TRISH MEEHAN	Olwen Fouere
GARDA	Andrew Bennett
LOGAN / BOY AT BUS STOP	Michael Coonan
CLOAKROOM ATTENDANT	Hilda Fay
KONIGSBERG	Carl Duering
MICHELLE	Nuala O'Neill
WOMAN IN DRESSING GOWN	Laurie Morton
MACK (OLD MAN)	Eamon Hunt
LISA	Lesley Conroy
HEADMISTRESS	Marie MacDermottroe
JUNIOR	Mark Dunne
OLD MAN IN BOOKIES	Derry Power
BARMAN / TEDDY	Kevin Hely
BOUNCER THREE	Tommy O'Neill
TEACHER	Sean Madden

The Filmmakers

Director and Writer	Conor McPherson
Producer	Robert Walpole
Executive Producer for the BBC	David M. Thompson
Executive Producer for the Irish Film Board	Rod Stoneman
Executive Producer for Radio Telefis Eireann	Clare Duignan
Associate Producer	Dominic Drumgoole
Associate Producer	Jan Roldanus
Director of Photography	Oliver Curtis BSC
Casting	Maureen Hughes
Casting	Deirdre O'Kane
Casting	Gail Stevens
Costume Designer	Kathy Strachan
Music	The Plague Monkeys
Editor	Emer Reynolds
Production Designer	Luana Hanson